WITHDRAWN

DATE DUE

TWAYNE'S WORLD AUTHORS SERIES
A Survey of the World's Literature

FRANCE

Maxwell A. Smith, Guerry Professor of French, Emeritus
The University of Chattanooga
Former Visiting Professor in Modern Languages
The Florida State University
EDITOR

Jacques Maritain

TWAS 474

Jacques Maritain

JACQUES MARITAIN

By JOHN M. DUNAWAY

Mercer University

TWAYNE PUBLISHERS
A DIVISION OF G. K. HALL & CO., BOSTON

Library of Congress Cataloging in Publication Data

Dunaway, John M
  Jacques Maritain.

  (Twayne's world authors series; TWAS 474: France)
  Bibliography: p. 164-69.
  Includes index.
  1.   Maritain, Jacques, 1882-1973.
B2430.M34D86   184   77-24189
ISBN 0-8057-6315-5

MANUFACTURED IN THE UNITED STATES OF AMERICA

To Trish with gratitude

Contents

About the Author

A native Georgian, John Dunaway received his academic degrees at Emory and Duke universities in French language and literature. He has written a monograph on the French-American novelist Julien Green for the University Press of Kentucky, in addition to articles and reviews on modern French literature. Mr. Dunaway is chairman of the Department of Modern Foreign Languages at Mercer University in Macon, Georgia, where he has taught since 1972.

Preface

Although it is a very great challenge to attempt to present a writer whose work combines the breadth and depth of a Jacques Maritain, I think it rather an advantage to be given this commission without either the formal training of a philosopher or the personal experience of being a Catholic. It is appropriate in a very real sense that Maritain should be presented by a non-Catholic and a nonphilosopher, for he is more than a philosopher for us today; he has brought to widely diverse realms of modern culture an intellectual honesty and a love for truth that have renewed our vision of man's highest ideals.

As a student of French literature, I was originally introduced to Jacques Maritain through his first book on aesthetics, *Art and Scholasticism* (1920), and then through the journals of Julien Green, the French-American novelist who was a longtime friend of the Maritains. Naturally, my interest in him is first and foremost concerned with his aesthetics and criticism, and these are the aspects of his work that I should like to emphasize in this study, along with his influence among men of letters during his career. In fact, there is a whole segment of Maritain's reading public who knew him primarily in this context.

I have also attempted, however, to summarize the most important teachings of Maritain. Chapters 2 - 4 concern his speculative philosophy, and his practical philosophy is outlined in Chapters 5 - 8 and 10. Chapter 9 explores a sort of *terra incognita,* namely, the question of Maritain's literary influence.

Translations of Maritain's books are of a highly uneven quality, and I have used the original versions in most cases. A number of his books, of course, were first written in English. The quotations used in the text here are almost exclusively in English, whether my translation or others'. The date of publication listed with titles is the date of the original publication, whether in French or English.

It has been my good fortune, in working on this book, to have the assistance of many people who should not go unacknowledged. Wallace Fowlie was an unfailing source of fresh ideas and always showed faith in me. It is a privilege to thank him for his support. I owe a special debt of gratitude to Joseph W. Evans, Francis

Fergusson, John Howard Griffin, and Cornelia Borgerhoff for their warm encouragement and generous help. I am very grateful to Eveline Garnier, Caroline Gordon, Allen Tate, Marshall McLuhan, Robert Speaight, and Father J. Stanley Murphy for their correspondence during this project. I should also like to thank the faculty research committee of Mercer University for making it possible for me to work at the Jacques Maritain Center at the University of Notre Dame and at Princeton University. To D. C. Bunn of the Stetson Memorial Library at Mercer I express my thanks for the books he made available through interlibrary loan.

JOHN M. DUNAWAY

Mercer University

Chronology

1882   November 18. Born in Paris to Paul and Geneviève Favre Maritain.

1898   Education at the Lycée Henri IV, where he befriends Ernest Psichari.

1900   Studies at Sorbonne. Meets Charles Péguy. Atmosphere of narrow empiricism leads to spiritual despair.

1901   Meets Raïssa Oumansoff, young Russian Jewess, at Sorbonne. Attends lectures by Henri Bergson at Collège de France. Rediscovery of "sense of the absolute."

1904   November 26. Marries Raïssa Oumansoff.

1905   Receives degree *agrégation de philosophie,* which qualifies him to teach in lycées. Meets Léon Bloy.

1906   June 11. Baptism of Jacques, Raïssa, and Véra Oumansoff as Roman Catholics. Bloy serves as godfather.

1906-   Studies in Heidelberg with biologist Hans Driesch. Begins
1908   compiling *Dictionnaire de la vie pratique* and an orthographic dictionary for Hachette publishers.

1908   Spring. Returns to Paris. Continues work for Hachette.

1910   June. First philosophical essay "La Science moderne et la raison," appears in *La Revue de Philosophie.* In September, begins reading Aquinas, whose *Summa* is a "deliverance, a flood of light," for Maritain.

1912   Teaches first philosophy course, at Collège Stanislas, Paris.

1913   Publishes first book, *La Philosophie bergsonienne, études critiques.*

1914   Becomes professor of philosophy at the Institut Catholique de Paris.

1917-   Corresponds with Pierre Villard, officer in French Army
1918   who is in spiritual turmoil.

1918   June. Pierre Villard dies in battle. Leaves family fortune to Charles Maurras and Maritain, whom he sees as guardians of the "intellectual and moral heritage" of France.

1919   Organization of first Thomist study groups. Versailles.

1921   First annual Thomist lecture retreat.

1923   Thanks to Villard's legacy, Maritain buys house at Meudon which is to become a center devoted to fostering growth of spirituality among intellectuals and artists of the time.

1926   Crisis of L'Action Française, reactionary publication of Maurras' political group. Papal condemnation of movement. Maritain, whose name has been associated with Maurras, disavows any relation with L'Action Française.

1927   *Primauté du spirituel (The Things That Are Not Caesar's)* signals the beginning of period of political and social involvement.

1930s   Builds reputation of political liberalism on issues such as Italian invasion of Ethiopia, Spanish Civil War, anti-Semitism.

1940–
1945   Teaches in Canada and United States at universities of Toronto and Chicago, Notre Dame, and Columbia.

1945   Appointed French Ambassador to the Vatican by de Gaulle. During his work in Rome he becomes friend of Monsignor Giovanni Montini, future Pope Paul VI.

1948   Teaches at Princeton University.

1960   Death of Raïssa Maritain.

1961   Returns to France. Retires to Toulouse to live with Little Brothers of Jesus, Dominican monastic order.

1973   April 28. Death of Maritain at Toulouse.

CHAPTER 1

Maritain the Man and His Vocation

I *The Philosopher in the World*

NICOLAI Berdiaev, the Russian Orthodox thinker whose Paris
apartment was the site of many interdenominational gatherings
during the late 1920s and 1930s, was visibly impressed with a certain
French Catholic philosopher who soon began to play a prominent
role in the discussions. The description of Jacques Maritain that is
found in Berdiaev's autobiography is a perceptive commentary on
the often puzzling character of this eloquent disciple of Thomas
Aquinas. "He is very sensitive to new modern tendencies. But
curiously enough, this has no effect on his philosophy. His
sensibility relates especially to the arts—in which he is very involved
—to mysticism, the philosophy of culture, and social problems. It
is he who first introduced Thomism into culture."[1]

Jacques Maritain was fond of using Saint Paul's idea of the
Christian's call to be in the world while not of the world. The
distinction is an altogether appropriate one, for Maritain has always
dealt in such paradoxes, and it is a useful key to bear in mind in
assessing the successive stands on diverse issues that one sees in the
development of this modern philosopher's career. Significantly, the
full French title of Maritain's epistemological study *The Degrees of
Knowledge* (1932) begins with the expression "distinguish to unite,"
an indication of the importance of paradox in the writer's intellectual method. But paradox is not confined to the writings of Maritain,
largely because he chose to live out his philosophy in an eminently
existential way, rather than placidly composing his grand *summa* in
some remote ivory tower.

Ours is a century in which men are constantly confronted with
choices. Today, perhaps more than ever before, man realizes that
to live and not simply to exist, he must commit himself to something
greater than himself. And he must make his commitment known to
others. For us the most tragic destiny imaginable is that of Eliot's

13

hollow men, who are remembered "not as lost violent souls," but as "shape[s] without form . . . paralyzed force." They neither live nor die, since they cannot choose to stand for good or for ill, and thus they recall the souls in the vestibule of Dante's hell, who chase madly after an elusive banner that stands for nothing.

Jacques Maritain is perhaps not the first name one would mention in a list of committed *(engagé)* twentieth century writers, and yet much of his life he has been no less committed to political and social issues than a Sartre, a Camus, or a Malraux. "To write is a consequence of living," as Saint-Exupéry has said, and it is difficult to guess whether the future will prove Maritain's writings or the example of his life to be his greatest accomplishment.

The work of Jacques Maritain is existential in the larger sense that it arises out of his own existential situation. His wife Raïssa made this point in her journal with the force of deep conviction. "Everything that is in Jacques' work we have first lived in the form of a vital difficulty, in the form of experience—problems of art and morality, of philosophy, of faith, of prayer, of contemplation. All this has been given to us first of all to *live,* each according to his nature and according to God's grace."[2] The Aristotelian realism in which Thomism is grounded was perfectly suited to Maritain's personality, and it was only natural for the impact of his philosophy to consist largely in calling modern Christendom back to its secular vocation. In a 1965 letter addressed to the authors of a Thomist evaluation of contemporary philosophy, Maritain claims precedence in this matter of existential emphasis. "You have rightly noted that Gilson's insistence on the existential perspective of Thomism came chronologically *before* the invasion of contemporary existentialism. The same is true for me. It was in deepening our understanding of Saint Thomas that these things appeared to us; it had nothing to do with some kind of adaptation to the existentialist fashion."[3]

II *Youth and Background (1882 - 1901)*

Maritain was born into an atmosphere of liberal Protestantism that one might further describe as free thinking and skeptical. During his youth, Hippolyte Taine and Ernest Renan were the reigning authorities in French intellectual circles. The rigidly rationalist doctrines of positivism were everywhere acclaimed as the *sine qua non* of the intellectual elite. Paul Maritain was a prominent Paris lawyer who seems not to have had any decisive influence on his son's thinking. His religious sentiments were relatively neutral.

The mother of Jacques Maritain was Geneviève Favre, the daughter of the great statesman Jules Favre. Favre was one of the architects of the Third Republic, a forceful orator and member of the French Academy, and he fit admirably into the chronological niche of positivism. His daughter felt passionately that the ultimate salvation of France lay in the hands of the intellectual elite and that religion had no place in the struggle. Inevitably, the young Maritain's innate spiritual fervor was channeled toward the social issues of the time. In his memoirs, Maritain quotes a fragment of a letter his mother had saved from the time of his adolescence. It is addressed to the family gardener, the most immediate representative of the proletariat, for Jacques seems, at this age, to be eager to devote his life to the working class.

I will be a socialist and live for the revolution . . . . It is an enormous debt . . . that I owe the proletariat . . . . It is for this reason that at this moment an uneasiness and a remorse enter into all that I do, into the joy I feel in learning. And certainly, all I can think and know I will devote to the proletariat and to humanity: I will use it entirely to prepare the revolution, to advance to some small degree the happiness and education of humanity.[4]

Later Maritain took a dim view of the revolutionary rhetoric that infuses this early letter, but the love of the working class professed in his adolescence was authentic, and it reflects the intensity of Maritain's social concerns throughout his career.

At the Lycée Henri IV, Maritain continued to study under the influence of scientism and socialism. Indeed, as fortune would have it, his closest friend at school—and one of the dearest friends of his lifetime, Ernest Psichari—was the grandson of Ernest Renan. Psichari and Maritain were inseparable during these years, and their ideas and feelings were equally close. But by the time the two reached the Sorbonne, Maritain had entered an agonizing crisis in his intellectual and spiritual development. He seemed to thirst for something beyond the answers to the human situation that he heard from the positivists.

III   *The Sorbonne (1901 - 1906)*

In order to appreciate the frustration that was in store for Maritain's inborn spiritual yearning, we must realize what tyranny of the mind was exercised by positivism during his youth. The example of Claudel, even though he predates Maritain a bit, is not without its parallels at the end of the nineteenth century. Claudel referred to his years at the Lycée Louis le Grand as "the sad years" because of the pervasive influence of the great skeptic Renan. And when on graduation day he was to receive academic honors, it was a nightmare come true when he was obliged to receive the prizes from the hand of none other than Renan, the hand he referred to as "la main du diable."

In this period of metaphysical anguish, Maritain met another student at the Sorbonne who shared his hunger for a fuller discovery of ultimate truth. Raïssa Oumansoff, daughter of Russian Jewish immigrants, first encountered Jacques Maritain when he was soliciting support for a protest movement against the treatment of Russian socialist students—an altogether appropriate beginning for their life together, for Raïssa would soon find herself supporting her husband in countless philosophical debates and social controversies. Raïssa herself was to become a poet and writer of some importance and doubtless was one of the principal reasons for her husband's lifelong interest in poetry. And in her diary, which Maritain published after her death, she is revealed as a moving example of the life of contemplation and self-surrender.

The depth of metaphysical despair in which the young couple were brought together is attested to by a promise they made to each other that if they failed to find the answer to the apparent meaninglessness of life within one year, they would both commit suicide. Predictably, this radical commitment to the quest for ultimate truth was ill received at the Sorbonne, but thanks to the suggestion of their socialist friend Charles Péguy, the couple began to attend the public lectures that Henri Bergson was giving at the Collège de France. Péguy, Psichari, Georges Sorel, and Jacques and Raïssa were among the growing group of young intellectuals whom Bergson led to a rediscovery of the "sense of the absolute." Dispelling the antimetaphysical prejudices of positivism, he liberated in them an intellectual urge for the spiritual realm. Perhaps even more significantly, Bergson's theory of intuition was achieving a rehabilitation of the intellectual respectability of metaphysical thought.

Because of Bergson's lectures, Maritain was saved from absolute despair and married Raïssa in 1904. Having found a measure of intellectual consolation, the two now met a person who was to give them their first living example of a soul totally abandoned to God's will. The encounter was a decisive one. The Maritains first discovered Léon Bloy through his writings. When in 1905 they visited the fiery, prophetic "thankless beggar" *(le mendiant ingrat),* their lives were changed forever. Living in incredible poverty, totally devoted to a life of prayer, suffering, and writing books that were never read, Bloy was the uncompromising witness of the call to sainthood. One of his most famous sayings—("There is only one sadness: not to be a saint")—was a beautiful expression of the state of mind of many young intellectuals of the period.

On June 11, 1906, Jacques, Raïssa, and her sister Vera Oumansoff were baptized in the Roman Catholic faith with Léon Bloy as godfather. Raïssa's parents took it as a betrayal of their heritage and a personal rejection. But Geneviève Favre was truly shattered. What a shock for a mother who had envisioned her son as the disciple of Péguy (at that time still a militant atheist)! She had held up three models for him: his grandfather Jules Favre in politics, Péguy in religion, and Bergson in philosophy. Now she would depend on Péguy to undo the pernicious influence of Bloy in her son's life. This was an affront to the family's good name, and she never forgave Jacques for it.

IV   *The Vocation Renewed (1906 - 1919)*

Maritain has always been thankful that at this trying moment in their lives, he, Raïssa, and Vera were able to find a haven where they could work, study, and meditate in serenity, sorting out their problems and orienting themselves to a new way of life. The little family spent two years (1906 - 1908) in Heidelberg, where Jacques studied with the experimental biologist Hans Driesch. In Germany their quiet, contemplative existence was not disturbed by family and friends as it might have been in France.

Having earned his *agrégation de philosophie* in 1905, Maritain was qualified to teach in the French lycées, but he had no desire to do so without any guarantee of being allowed to teach according to his own philosophical persuasion. It was a stroke of fortune that about this time Hachette publishers gave him the assignments of compiling a "dictionary of practical life" and an orthographic dictionary. These tasks were not altogether unrelated to his work in philosophy and allowed him more intellectual independence than he would have found in teaching. By the time of his return to Paris in the spring of 1908, he was more strongly confirmed in the Catholic faith.

In Paris, Maritain proceeded with this work for Hachette and his own readings. At the time of his conversion, he had felt that there was probably a great gulf between his previous philosophical convictions and his newfound faith. In fact, he was prepared to sacrifice philosophy for the sake of his religion. Thus, when in 1910 he began to read the *Summa Theologiae* of Thomas Aquinas, Maritain had attempted to rid himself of his former intellectual baggage, and the seed of Saint Thomas's writings fell on fertile ground. It was as much a conversion experience as meeting Bloy had been, a joyous flood of enlightenment, and the definitive revelation of his life's vocation. "Woe unto me, should I not Thomize," he told himself as he realized that he had found his vocation and the master whose work he would perpetuate. "Jacques's vocation," wrote Raïssa in her memoirs, "shall have been to bring to light the vital forces of Thomism . . . to widen its frontiers while holding in the strictest fashion to its principles, to reinsert it into the existential reality of the movement of culture and philosophy."[5]

Maritain began teaching in 1912 at the Collège Stanislas in Paris, a Catholic school in which he felt free to teach his own version of philosophy. His philosophy course was a rather controversial one and contrasted sharply with the materialism taught at the lycées. Even in a Catholic secondary school, there was no small reaction when the professor announced that all his classes would begin with the recitation of an Ave Maria.

The young philosopher continued to generate consternation when his first book was published in 1913. Having been an avid disciple of Bergson during his years at the Sorbonne, Maritain now appeared to make a complete *volte-face*. In *La Philosophie bergsonienne,* he warned against the dangers of Bergson's philosophical system. He further developed his thesis in public lectures at the Institut Catholique de Paris in the spring of 1913.

These lectures were quite a sensation, attracting a lively, vocal public; and Maritain's insistence on the authority of Saint Thomas was often inflammatory. The audience was witnessing the first public manifesto of the Catholic renaissance, one of the great cultural movements of the first half of our century.

During World War I, Maritain was professor of philosophy at the Institut Catholique and continued writing and lecturing. He tried repeatedly to enter the armed services but was rejected for reasons of health. In order to make a greater contribution to France's war effort, he increased his teaching program and lectured on German philosophy and its tendencies that led toward totalitarianism. The war years brought much personal grief to the Maritains, with the death of several of their closest friends, among them Psichari and Péguy (both in battle), Bloy, and Father Clérissac, their first spiritual director.

Perhaps the greatest event of the war years for Maritain was meeting Pierre Villard. Villard was an officer in the French Army who was introduced to Maritain through his writings. He was searching his way through a grave spiritual crisis and found consolation in his correspondence with Maritain. After Villard had died a heroic death in battle, it was discovered that he had willed the greater portion of his family's rather large fortune to Charles Maurras and Maritain. The bequest proved a mixed blessing. It gave Maritain the financial independence that was necessary for him to devote his time to promoting the philosophy of Saint Thomas, but it also played a part in leading him to one of the greatest crises of his early career.

V Meudon and the "Jours de Soleil" (1919 - 1940)

Between 1919 and 1940, Maritain was able to give up teaching as a livelihood (although he still lectured at the Institut Catholique from time to time) and to devote most of his time to his writing. He used part of the Villard bequest to purchase a house in Meudon, a suburban town between Paris and Versailles. Here he established a center for the promotion of Thomist studies. With the help of Raïssa and Vera, he received groups of intellectuals on Sunday afternoons, and the meetings soon evolved into Thomist seminars and attracted widely divergent intellectual and artistic types. There were also annual Thomist lecture retreats, which were attended by very great

numbers of participants. The house at 10, rue du Parc in
Meudon became a mecca for people of various backgrounds
and professions who were searching for the kind of spiritual
food that sustained the Maritains. The quiet strength of Jacques
Maritain encountered in person is reflected in the large number
of conversions and religious vocations at Meudon during these
years.

The crisis in which Maritain was involved, in part through
Pierre Villard's generosity, was that of Charles Maurras' political
group and its official publication, both known as L'Action
Française. Although Maritain was never a member of the party,
he was a friend of Maurras and was thrown into more direct
association with him by the Villard gift.

Maritain was almost exclusively concerned at this time (the
1920s) with speculative philosophy and had lost almost all his
youthful interest in political matters. He was unfamiliar with
most of Maurras' writing and thus was largely unaware of the
dangers in becoming associated with the name Maurras. Charles
Maurras was an intransigent royalist, an ultraconservative
nationalist, an anticommunist, anti-Semitic advocate of strict law
and order. His political party was popular among conservative
Catholics, despite his own unabashed positivism. Maritain's
spiritual director Father Clérissac was also a great admirer of
Maurras and had a large part in associating Maritain with the
movement.

In August of 1926, Pope Pius XI published a condemnation of
Maurras' periodical L'Action Française. It was an important
awakening for Maritain. He publicly disavowed any association
—real or supposed—with L'Action Française and its ideals. And
he was impelled by this experience to begin elaborating (on the
basis of Aquinas, as always) the Christian's responsibility in the
secular realm. The first fruit of his labor was Primauté du
spirituel, or The Things That Are Not Caesar's (1927), in which
he refuted Maurras' motto of "politics first." Other evidences
of the new political emphasis in his work were the Letter on
Independence (1935) and Integral Humanism (1936), his
landmark work on social and political philosophy.

In the troubled decade of the 1930s Maritain was still writing
voluminously, and his gatherings at Meudon were at the height
of their popularity, and hence very time-consuming. In addition
to keeping abreast of artistic and literary developments, he was

editing a series of books for Plon publishers. But the significantly new realm of his activities was the social and political
controversies in which he began to involve himself. He was
instrumental in directing the Catholic weekly *Sept,* which repeatedly took dangerous stands on current issues until its suppression
in 1937. He collaborated in numerous manifestoes that appeared
at this time. One of the most important was entitled "Pour le
bien commun" ("For the Common Good") which appeared in
1934 following the Stavisky affair and widespread rioting.
Maritain and fifty-one other Catholic intellectuals, seeing the
danger of a fascist takeover in France, deplored the injustices of
both left and right and advocated instead a pluralist, humanist
political order. This sociopolitical ideal, which valued justice and
human well-being above partisan sympathies, was characteristic
of all Maritain's political involvements and is enunciated in the
Letter on Independence. It is again evident in his refusal to
endorse Franco's White Crusade in the Spanish Civil War and
in his condemnation of the Italian invasion of Ethiopia in 1935.
Both these stands were in direct conflict with the majority
opinion of French Catholics.

The crisis of L'Action Française was a moment of great
personal anguish for Maritain, who recognized that he had made
some serious errors in judgment, and it cost him the loss of some
highly valued friendships. But it was providential in that it
helped involve him in secular problems, an emphasis which for
a "neoscholastic" philosopher has appeared incongruous to
many. "Jacques has always been in the fight—and, with this,
time for meditation has been granted him. He has had to write
his books on the urgency of the moment, and of this urgency he
has always been terribly aware. The sudden breaking of faith
into his soul scattered all his plans for methodical work."[6]

VI *American Exile (1940 - 1945)*

At the time of the German invasion of France in 1940, the
Maritains were in Toronto, where Jacques was lecturing at the
Pontifical Institute of Medieval Studies. He had already made
other visits for this purpose, thanks to the invitations of his
friend, the great Thomist historian of philosophy, Etienne
Gilson. Because of Jacques's well-known stand against fascism
and because of Raïssa's and Vera's Jewish parentage, it was out

of the question for the family to return to France. Although they had enjoyed their visits to this continent and were fond of the United States, an imposed exile was a deep and tragic sorrow. Maritain, like many other Frenchmen in exile, devoted a great amount of time and effort to the freeing of his country. He spoke often on "Voice of America" broadcasts in support of the Resistance movement. In *France, My Country, Through the Disaster* (1941), he attempted to restore moral support for the French cause, both here and in his fallen country. He edited several series of books that shared his humanist ideals, and was instrumental in the founding of the Ecole Libre des Hautes Etudes (known as the only Free French university during the war), of which he was later president. As usual, he continued to teach and lecture, traveling, among other places, to the Univerisities of Toronto and Chicago, and to Columbia, Yale, and Notre Dame.

Maritain's writing during the war was primarily concerned with practical philosophy. His humanist concept of education is outlined in *Education at the Crossroads* (1943), and *Christianity and Democracy* (1943) reveals his notion of true democracy as a political system inspired by divine providence. His stand against the horrors of racism and anti-Semitism was also an important commitment during his years in the United States. Many of these ideas are briefly summed up in his *Reflections on America* (1958), in which he not only reveals himself as one who has grown to love America but also points out with sharp perceptiveness the strengths and weaknesses of this country. The informal style of this book, which grew out of three seminars he gave at Chicago on the American character, gives it an appealing tone of spontaneity. As in the case of his letter to Jean Cocteau (*Réponse à Jean Cocteau,* or *Art and Faith,* 1926), the informality of the style actually enhances its philosophical content.

VII   *Rome (1945 - 1948)*

At the end of World War II, President de Gaulle asked Maritain to serve as the French Ambassador to the Holy See. It was not a position that he would have chosen, and Raïssa, he knew, would be burdened by the endless social duties that it would entail. However, the family decided that it was a commission that could not be refused, and so the Maritains lived from 1945 to 1948 in Rome. Jacques, of course, did not allow his diplomatic duties to still his pen and pursued the general direction of social and political philosophy that was the keynote of his work throughout the thirties and forties.

One of the more controversial issues in which he became embroiled was the worker-priest movement in France. During the war a few French priests, seeing so many laborers being deported to Germany, decided to join them in the work camps. Later, others were permitted to work in factories, thereby seizing a unique opportunity to share the plight of the poor and accomplish a unique apostolate among them. Maritain's support of the movement did not prevent its suppression by ecclesiastical authorities, but in 1965 the Vatican finally revoked its ban of the movement, allowing it to function with more careful supervision.

During his residence in Rome, Maritain made the acquaintance of one Giovanni Montini, who was later to become Pope Paul VI. The Vatican official was so profoundly influenced by the French philosopher that he has since called himself a disciple of Maritain and has even footnoted him in the encyclical *Populorum progressio* ("On the Development of Peoples"). Perhaps the greatest honor of Jacques Maritain's career came when Pope Paul, at the end of Vatican II, addressed a message to intellectuals of the world through Maritain and publicly embraced him in Saint Peter's Square.

VIII   *Princeton (1948 - 1961)*

At the conclusion of his term as ambassador in 1948, Maritain faced a difficult decision. For the first time in almost a decade, he was free to live again in his homeland. He, Raïssa, and Vera would undoubtedly be happier there. But Maritain sensed that his place was still in America. His influence in France was no longer what it had been before the war. Moreover, the generation of Americans who were going through Catholic colleges and universities in the 1940s looked upon him as the foremost thinker of their age. Maritain finally decided to accept Princeton President Harold Dodds' standing offer to become professor of philosophy there. It was his last teaching position.

At Princeton the Maritains were able to return to a life more suited to their contemplative needs. The war years and the years in Rome had been among their busiest times, and Raïssa especially had suffered from it. For her it was a consolation to have a few years in which she could give more time to prayer and meditation, the very bread of her life. Visitors to the house on Linden Lane have recounted that the family went to great lengths to reconstruct much of the atmosphere of the "jours de soleil" (sunlit days) at Meudon. And the artist André Girard even tried to assuage the Maritains' homesickness by painting murals depicting French scenes in some of the rooms.

Jacques's work during this period was prolific and diverse. In 1952 he gave the Mellon Lectures on the Fine Arts in Washington, D.C., which were soon published as *Creative Intuition in Art and Poetry* (1953). With *Art and Scholasticism* (1920), this is undoubtedly his most cherished work among writers and artists. It is the bible of Maritain's aesthetic thought. Another important book concerning art and letters was published in 1960, *The Responsibility of the Artist*.

Maritain wrote more in English during his Princeton years than at any other time of his career. Such important works as *Man and the State* (1951), *Creative Intuition in Art and Poetry, The Responsibility of the Artist, On the Philosophy of History* (1957), and *Reflections on America* were written originally in English. Maritain had chosen to make himself a very real presence in American culture, and his influence on Catholic thought and on art and letters was enormous.

After his retirement in 1952, Maritain remained professor emeritus at Princeton until his return to France in 1961. The serenity of the academic atmosphere was pleasing to him there, but the 1950s were also a time of personal trials and grief for the little family. Jacques was stricken by a severe heart attack in 1954, and Vera's struggle with heart disorders and cancer was a prolonged period of agony that finally ended in her death in 1959. Finally, during a visit to France in July of 1960, Raïssa was striken with cerebral thrombosis and never recovered. She died on November 4.

IX *Retirement with the Little Brothers (1961 - 1973)*

Left completely alone at the age of seventy-nine, Maritain might never have recovered from the loss of these two souls who had shared his life for a half century. Fortunately, there was a home for him where he could find the same gentle solicitude balanced by an understanding of his need for privacy, both of which he had enjoyed with Raïssa and Vera. This home he found in Toulouse, among the Little Brothers of Jesus, a Dominican monastic order that follows a rule of discipline created by Father Charles de Foucauld. The Little Brothers live in poverty and do exhausting physical work among common laborers. They live in small groups and share among themselves their particular ritual devotions but make no attempts to evangelize by word of mouth. Their lives are their silent testimony.

At Toulouse, Maritain wrote still more important works—his memoirs, *Carnet de Notes* (1965); *The Peasant of the Garonne* (1966); and *On the Church of Christ* (1970)—and edited *Raïssa's Journal* (1963) from notes that were discovered after her death. His most important lectures to the Little Brothers, along with other essays, were published posthumously in 1973 as *Approches sans entraves*.

The aging philosopher had retired from the world in the 1960s, and although the Second Vatican Council gave official sanction to many of the causes for which he had labored so long, he was no longer a major philosophical influence in French culture. At the Sorbonne, most students were concentrating their attention on Claude Lévi-Strauss and other structuralist proponents of the anthropological explanation of man. Those who were interested in theology often mentioned the name of the late Father Pierre Teilhard de Chardin with great respect and enthusiasm.

The publication of *The Peasant of the Garonne* in 1966, then, was the occasion of the last great furor in which Maritain became involved. Most of his followers, who had found in him a champion of liberalizing influences in the Catholic church, were appalled at what they considered a complete reversal of positions. He seemed to be wary of the same developments in Vatican II that his work had helped to bring about. Yet Maritain himself called the book the crowning of his thought. It caused such a sensation that it led the bestseller lists for months in France and was widely sold in the United States and elsewhere.

Although he announced with the publication of *The Peasant of the Garonne* that it was his last book, two more works were published before his death: *On the Grace and Humanity of Jesus* (1967) and *On the Church of Christ*. Both these studies were outgrowths of his controversial work on the *aggiornamento,* or "updating" of the Church.

In 1969, Maritain was granted special permission to enter the monastic order of the Little Brothers of Jesus. He said that he had been a rebel all his life, and it was now time for him to live the life of obedience. Revolt had indeed been one of his trademarks: against the scientism of his mother's generation, against the philosophy of his own master Bergson, often against the political stands of the Catholic majority, and finally even against those who thought they were carrying on his ideals. During these last years Maritain was physically frail and weak, but those who were allowed to visit him were amazed at the lively awareness of his intellectual faculties. At the door of his simple cabin his visitors were confronted with a little sign which read: "Here [lives] an aged hermit arrived at the end of his life. If his head is no longer worth anything, as well leave him to his dreams. If you believe he still has something to do then have the charity to observe the rule imposed by his work: NOT MORE THAN A HALF-HOUR OF CONVERSATION."[7] Thus, at the age of ninety, and until his death on April 28, 1973, of a heart attack, Maritain continued in his vocation of making the intelligence a "subtly flashing sword in the defense of faith."[8] His last act as a writer was to autograph a book for a recently released convict who had discovered his writings in prison.

CHAPTER 2

Metaphysics

MARITAIN'S speculative philosophy may be best understood by beginning with his metaphysics. *A Preface to Metaphysics,*[1] which he first published in 1934, is a concise outline of the Thomist ontology. Subtitled *Seven Lectures on Being,* it is one of the most important books of Maritain precisely because its content is so vitally fundamental to all his other philosophical works. It is also an exciting intellectual experience in itself for its admirable treatment of problems of universal philosophical importance.

I *The Need for Thomist Metaphysics*

The introductory lecture offers a persuasive argument for the necessity of a "living Thomism," the only philosophy capable of saving intellectual and human values in the speculative and practical orders. The chaotic state of contemporary philosophy Maritain attributes to an increasing tendency to disdain metaphysical knowledge in favor of the phenomenological sciences.

Every question of science or philosophy has two basic aspects: it is both a "mystery" and a "problem." It is a problem in as much as it is a puzzle for the intellect to solve; such is the nature of purely empirical knowledge. Yet the act of knowing also involves an aspect of mystery. The intellect *becomes* what is other than itself—it assimilates what is outside itself in a mysterious way. This mystery, which is contained in the object of knowledge, is too pregnant with meaning to be wholly assimilated; it is absolutely comprehensible only to the mind of God. Metaphysics is a science in which the mystery aspect predominates over the problem aspect. Modern philosophy has been too unwilling to deal with the ontological problem except on an empirical, problem-oriented basis. And thus, for Maritain, the great error of modern philosophy lies in "treating

27

philosophy, metaphysics, wisdom—a category of knowledge in which *reverence* for the mystery of being is the highest factor—as . . . pre-eminently a problem to answer, a puzzle to solve" (PM, 9). "A philosophy unaware of mystery," he writes, "would not be a philosophy" (PM, 5).

Proceeding on the empirical method proper to the problem aspect of reality, modern philosophy has been characterized by the concept of progress by substitution which again is proper to the sciences of phenomena. A new doctrine gains credence to the point of replacing an older one, in the same fashion as the long line of scientific revolutions that have occurred throughout history. Just as the Copernican system replaced Ptolemaic astronomy, even so have we seen medieval philosophy rejected in favor of Descartes, Descartes in favor of Kant, Kant in favor of Bergson, and so on. "We have witnessed human reason gone astray and a captive to empiricism seeking wisdom more anxiously than ever before, yet failing to find it, because it has rejected the sense of mystery and has attempted to subject wisdom to the alien law of progress by substitution" (PM, 11). Such "progress" by substitution is antithetical to the science of being, according to Maritain, for "truth cannot be subjected to a chronological test" (PM, 3).

The concept of scientific progress which Maritain holds to be proper to the science of being is rather a progress "by a growing intimacy" (PM, 9). It is a progress attained through the deepening of principles inherent in the object of knowledge that do not change. Thomism, then, restores to philosophy the all-important continuity of tradition, the timeless truths of metaphysics that remain to be deepened and to grow in our understanding of them, but that cannot be replaced by new doctrines for the sake of their novelty.

II   *What Metaphysical Being Is Not*

Having thus stated his argument for the necessity of metaphysics in general and of Thomism in particular, Maritain proceeds in the second lecture, entitled "Counterfeit Metaphysical Coin," to demonstrate how modern philosophy has confused the issue of the proper subject of metaphysics. He takes it as a given that metaphysics is concerned with being. But the definition of being is the primary source of confusion, so that this chapter amounts to a careful exposition of what being, as the subject of metaphysics, is not.

The natural sciences, the empirical sciences of phenomena, have as their subject being as particularized, being as actualized, and as the "foundation of observable and measurable phenomena . . . in so far as it is involved in the sensible and changing corporeal world" (PM, 28). Common sense likewise is concerned with being, but here the metaphysical concept of being is veiled, masked by vagueness. Common sense perceives dimly the metaphysical concept of being without disengaging it and distinguishing it from other concepts. Common sense, says Maritain, is "a rough sketch of metaphysics, a vigorous and unreflective sketch drawn by the natural motion and spontaneous instincts of reason" (PM, 29). A third concept of being—"being divested of reality"—is the subject of logic. Maritain qualifies it as divested of reality because the logician is concerned only with being as it is perceived in the mind, or conceptual being—being, that is to say, only as it is involved in the process of reasoning. Since conceptual being cannot exist outside the mind, it cannot really exist. All this is as it should be. Maritain is not attempting to discredit the natural sciences, common sense, or logic. These are all viable modes of thought and have their own use. What he wants to make clear is the radical intellectual error involved in confusing the subject of metaphysics—being strictly as being— with these other concepts of being.

Finally, Maritain points out three notions of modern philosophy under the heading of "pseudo-being," all of which he attributes to a "misconceived and decadent logic." The fundamental flaw in Hegel's system, he suggests, was that Hegel forgot that being is a transcendental. Assuming that it was of a purely generic nature, he sought to reach an understanding of being as the supreme genus. And by the law of logical abstraction, he was obliged to identify being with nothingness, with nonentity. Another error, illustrated by Kant, was to consider logic as "a science of the laws and forms of a thought *divorced* from things and independent of them" (PM, 37). This concept of a pure form of thought created an artificial split between thought and things. Third, the Platonic or Scotist notion of metaphysics commits the error of separating metaphysics from existence, confining it to the description of essences. "When we affirm that the object of the intellect is being, an affirmation which displays the profound realism of Thomist philosophy, we do not stop short at essences. It is to existence itself that the intellect proceeds when it formulates within itself a judgement corresponding to what a thing is or is not outside the mind" (PM, 20 - 21).

It is for this reason that Maritain calls Thomism an existential philosophy. Years before the new wave of enthusiasm for Jean-Paul Sartre and Albert Camus, Maritain was pointing to a thirteenth-century philosopher as the most important existential thinker for today's problems.

The Thomist metaphysician . . . must not be exclusively an intellect . . . . He must be keenly and profoundly aware of sensible objects. And he should be plunged into existence, steeped ever more deeply in it by a sensuous and aesthetic perception as acute as possible, and by experiencing the suffering and struggles of real life, so that aloft in the third heaven of natural understanding he may feed upon the intelligible substance of things. (PM, 23 - 24)

III *Defining Metaphysical Being*

It would be intellectual suicide for a student of metaphysics to consider being as one of the nonmetaphysical concepts that Maritain has enumerated in his second lecture. The next chapter, then, directs the reader's attention to "The True Subject of Metaphysics," which is "being disengaged and isolated from the sensible quiddity, being viewed as such and set apart in its pure intelligible values" (PM, 19). All things are permeated with being and murmur it for the hearing of the intellect. But metaphysical being is not perceived by everyone. Only those who have reached the necessary degree of intellectual spirituality are attuned to the music uttered by the fullness of intelligibility.

The perception of metaphysical being is an intuitive experience, one that calls forth some of Maritain's most elegantly lyrical passages of philosophical prose. It is "a very simple sight, superior to any discursive reasoning . . . a sight whose content and implications no words of human speech can exhaust or adequately express and in which in a moment of decisive emotion, as it were, of spiritual conflagration, the soul is in contact, a living, penetrating and illuminating contact, with a reality which it touches and which takes hold of it" (PM, 46).

Maritain's description of this intuitive experience is portrayed in such affective terms as to suggest something akin to Bergsonian intuition. Indeed, the intuition of metaphysical being is a grace, a gift bestowed on those who have ears to hear. And he compares it to the sudden intuition of one's own individual existence, which can take on the glow of a mystical grace or the tragic sense of the loss of innocence—such as one finds, for example, in Julien Green's account of the experience.

> Every man has known the peculiar instant when one feels sharply divided from the rest of the world, by the fact of being one's own self and not part of what surrounds us. . . . It was the melancholy hour when the first person singular put in an appearance in human life to occupy the center of the stage and stay there jealously till the last gasp. Of course I was happy later, but not as I used to be in the Eden from which we are chased by the fiery angel called Me.[2]

But there is one essential difference between a Bergsonian intuition (such as Green's) and the intuition of metaphysical being: namely, the intellectual quality of the latter. Bergson denied the intellectual aspect. But for Maritain, intuition—such as he describes—is a vital function of the intellect. Just as in his theory of creative poetic intuition—the central experience of the artist—Maritain here preserves a balance between the intellectual and affective aspects of the intelligence.

The intuition of metaphysical being is the most important requisite for a metaphysician, according to Maritain. It cannot be produced by a subtle method or technique; it was precisely for this reason that Kant missed such an experience. There are certain other experiences that can prepare us for it, such as Bergson's intuition of duration and Heidegger's anguish. But these cannot induce the metaphysical intuition of being, for it is a leap of faith that the intelligence takes in its sovereign freedom.

The heart of the matter, what Maritain has to say concerning being as such, is contained in the long fourth lecture. First, being is essentially and intrinsically analogous in the sense that it is both manifold and one. It is manifold, polyvalent, because it finds itself manifested in the diversity of sensible matter, the many particularized things which *are,* which have being. And yet being as such is still undivided, it is one. Each particularized thing has to varying degrees the same single quality of being.

This concept of being in which things partake is characterized by the polarity of essence-existence. Wherever there is being, there is both a nature or "essence" of what is and the action, so to speak, of being, or "existence." The two extremes of the polarity must not be isolated; indeed, in the mind of God this ideal distinction does not exist.

Because the metaphysical reality apprehended by the intuition of being is too pregnant with meaning to be conveyed by the term being, it overflows and generates concepts by which the metaphysician becomes better aware of the overwhelming richness of being. Being perceived in its various aspects, then, gives the transcendentals: unity, truth, goodness. Being is essentially overflowing, and wherever there is being, there is necessarily tendency and love. In all corporeal being, tendency or love produces motion and change, since being, in perfecting itself, must move toward a quality outside itself that gives it perfection. But in God, who is being itself, there is no motion or change, for "if the being that loves *is* Himself intellection and love, as God is, when He knows and loves Himself, he does not perfect Himself, acquires no new perfection. But He overflows all the same. And this overflow is His being itself" (PM, 73—Maritain's italics). It is in this sense of God as the overflowing fullness of being that Maritain sheds new light on the familiar biblical statements: *Ego sum qui sum* and *Deus caritas est*.

IV   *The Metaphysician's Mode of Knowing*

What the metaphysician learns about being, Maritain says, is attained through an objective light or mode of knowledge that he calls "intensive visualization" or "intensive abstraction." He prefers the former term in order to avoid confusing it with extensive abstraction, a prescientific mode of knowledge that is very similar to the knowledge that common sense has of "vague being." This distinction he borrows from Cajetan and John of Saint Thomas. Intensive visualization is "a visualization in which knowledge is completely immaterialized, that is to say, the object is visualized *sine omni materia*" (PM, 79). The physical sciences, mathematics, and metaphysics, respectively, are characterized by modes of knowledge that are in ascending order of intensive visualization or abstraction. The most immaterial mode of knowledge, the metaphysician's objective light, is the only one capable of penetrating "the intelligible mystery . . . that in being which is deeper than the intelligibility tied to the perception of the outer senses or the intelligibility tied to imaginative intuition" (PM, 83).

The abstraction of which Maritain is speaking must not be understood, he warns, in a totally negative sense. To abstract, literally, is to draw something out from something else in which it is embedded, not to discard or destroy that from which it is thus taken. What makes the process seem all the more difficult is that the loftiest, most immaterial object of knowledge—metaphysical being—is "that which is most universal and commonest" (PM, 86), common to all things and constantly present. Metaphysical being is "hidden being," a vastly rich intelligible object that is difficult to know by virtue of its very nearness and omnipresence. We take it for granted in the same way that we have no intimate acquaintance with persons whom we see every day. The mystery of being is hidden in the commonest of little words, the verb "to be," which we use with a superficial impression of understanding.

V First Principles

Among the first principles of speculative reason, Maritain briefly defines four (identity, sufficient reason, finality, and causality) and mentions other self-evident principles that could be profitably elaborated, using the Thomist method. According to the principle of identity, each being is what it is. Rather than presenting an innocuous tautology, this statement lays the very foundation of Aristotelian-Thomist metaphysics. "What is posited outside its causes exercises an activity, an energy which is existence itself" (PM, 93). And since existence cannot be fully comprehended within the mind, Maritain is speaking of coherent extramental existence, existence that is not dependent upon logic or thought.

Since the intellect is made for being and since being is the sufficient good of the intellect, Maritain asserts, whatever renders an object intelligible is that in virtue of which it is. This statement is what he calls the principle of sufficient reason, and he further enunciates this second principle of metaphysics in these terms: *"Everything which is, to the extent to which it is, possesses a sufficient reason for its being;* that is to say, . . . it is capable of explaining itself to the intellect, though not necessarily to *our* intellect; *whatever is, is intelligibly determined; whatever is, has that whereby it is*" (PM, 99; Maritain's italics).

The third principle of metaphysics, the principle of finality, is the one to which Maritain devotes the most exhaustive discussion. It has to do essentially with the dynamic aspect of contingent being. Since God has uncreated, self-existent being, His being does not require completion by potency. Thus, the principles of finality and causality apply only to contingent, created being, where action is distinct from the agent. Most succinctly, the finality of being is expressed by the following double statement: Potency essentially refers to act, and every agent acts in view of an end. Being does not act indeterminately. And since there is an end envisioned in all human action, the act must already exist in the mind as knowledge before it is carried out physically. "The dynamism of being presupposes knowledge and thought, the forming Word" (PM, 119).

With this principle in mind, Maritain is able to explain knowledge and love as analogous immanent actions in man. Both knowledge and love enable the agent to become something other than himself and thus to perfect the knowing-loving subject in himself. Both prefigure the union of the subject with the ultimate object of love and knowledge. Likewise, the principle of finality illuminates the notion of chance or fortuity. Chance appears to contradict finality, for it implies that something can occur without any end to determine it. But for Maritain, as for Aquinas, chance events are explained by conflicting lines of causation that intersect at a given point. "They have no unity, but are merely the coincidence of a manifold. . . . The sole unity they can possess is in thought" (PM, 126).

Finally, Maritain considers the principle of causality. It is in this context, he claims, that the metaphysician is most aware of the profound mystery of being. The creative act, the process by which something passes from nothingness into being, is the ultimate mystery for the philosopher. The contemplation of the creative act naturally gives rise to the eminently self-evident principle of causality: Every contingent being has a cause.

Since this is only an introduction to metaphysics, Maritain does not proceed beyond the first four principles of speculative reason. He does end the book, however, by alluding to several of the other subordinate axioms and by suggesting that the field is open for contemporary metaphysicians to develop and comment on them. *A Preface to Metaphysics* is thus a preliminary charting of the land that needs to be explored by modern Thomists. It is also a concise presentation of the foundations of Maritain's thought and is indispensable for an understanding of his other writings. For in each field of intellectual inquiry he entered, he constantly referred to the principles of Thomist metaphysics for the point of departure, thus imparting a basic unity to all his thought.

CHAPTER 3

Epistemology

U NLIKE *A Preface to Metaphysics, The Degrees of Knowl-edge*[1] is a book of imposing size that aims to survey the entire extent of its subject. The word "integral" has immense significance for Maritain; witness the title of his first great text of political philosophy, *Integral Humanism*. For him, a philosopher has an inescapable obligation to consider the subject of his particular field of inquiry as a whole. This is one of the great strengths of Thomism, and this is one sense in which Maritain calls Thomism a "realistic" philosophy. It examines reality in all its richness; it is characterized by an attitude of openness, even of humility toward what is real. Rather than taking its place alongside all the other philosophical systems as an alternative way of seeing reality, Thomism undergirds them all. One does not become a Thomist by choosing this one view from among "the emporium of systems," just as one chooses a new pair of shoes in a shoe store. It is rather, a matter of "allowing oneself to be taught by the whole range of human thought, in order not to neglect anything of that which is" (DK, xiii). The extreme preponderance of Aristotle and Aquinas in the scholastic tradition is explained not by a blind fidelity to them on the part of their disciples, but by "their supreme docility to the lessons of the real" (DK, iii). Because of its superior intellectual integrity, then, Thomism "is not a system, an artifact, it is a spiritual organism" (DK, xiii), one which grows with the assimilation of new ideas, rather than being superseded by them.

I *Philosophy and Experimental Science*

The Degrees of Knowledge is Maritain's definitive work in epistemology, and it is in this Thomist spirit of openness to integral reality that it was written. The first part of the title, which is less often cited, is *Distinguish to Unite*. In *The Degrees of Knowledge,* the author has proposed a synthesis of knowledge, "starting with the experience of the physicist and ending with the experience of the contemplative" (DK, xi). It was a stroke of genius to combine in the title of his study the scholastic method of *distinguo* with the forward-looking intent of *uniting* tradition with the present, a movement that, as we have just observed, characterizes the growth of Thomism as a spiritual organism.

The scope of this book is extremely broad. It is divided into two main parts, the first of which establishes the degrees of rational knowledge; the second, the degrees of suprarational knowledge. In the first part, there is a constant concern on Maritain's part to define the relationship of philosophy and experimental science. He first distinguishes between the proper provinces of philosophy and experimental science. Then he takes care to demonstrate how vital it is for these two realms of thought to work cooperatively toward the goal of truth.

Maritain makes it very clear that for the Thomist, experimental science, while maintaining its autonomy within the limits of its own sphere of knowledge, is dependent upon philosophy. Science is concerned with the abstract, with "ideal constancies and supramomentary determinations" (DK, 24). It can predict for us what will happen in a given set of ideal circumstances, thanks to the intelligible necessity of scientific laws. But these laws can do no more than "express . . . the property or requirement of a certain ontological indivisible which of itself does not fall under the senses" (DK, 24 - 25). Whether scientific laws actually correspond to these individual, ontological nonobservables is problematical: "Statistical law," for example, "seems . . . to be a substitute at second hand for the intelligible necessities inscribed in the universal, which experimental science cannot quite succeed in deciphering" (DK, 27). In other words, the "contingencies of the singular escape science. The necessities of the universal are the proper objects of its grasp" (DK, 27).

Experimental science depends upon philosophy in principle, according to Maritain. That is to say, it does not need philosophy for the discovery or application of its laws. But it does depend on philosophy to explain and justify such laws. The axioms of science are statements that describe certain properties of ontological reality. But without philosophy, man would be unable to identify the ontological content upon which those axioms rest. "It is philosophy that determines the nature of the primary objects the scientists work on and, consequently, their own very nature, value and limits" (DK, 49).

"There is no science without first principles to which all our reasonings must be reduced" (DK, 49). The soul of a living man cannot be void. It will be filled with whatever gods he follows in his life, with whatever values in which he consciously or unconsciously invests his faith. Similarly, a living human intellect cannot be devoid of philosophy. The scientist, by the very practice of his discipline, operates on certain consciously or unconsciously accepted assumptions of a speculative order. Every science presupposes a certain philosophy. An experimental scientist, for example, works with an implicit faith in the metaphysical principle of causality.

In comparing the ancients' view of knowledge to the moderns', Maritain acknowledges that for the former, philosophy all too often overstepped its bounds and ended by rendering experimental science a confused jumble that was bound to collapse. However, he also points out the need for modern philosophy to catch up with the great leaping progress of modern experimental science. The metaphysics and philosophy of the ancients, insists Maritain, remain unaffected by the collapse of their scientific system, much as the soul remains unchanged when the body disintegrates. What Maritain is proposing, then, is a balanced synthesis of what is best in modern and ancient knowledge—a synthesis of scholastic philosophy and modern experimental science, in the same mold as Aquinas's synthesis of Aristotle and Christian theology.

II   The Problem of the Cartesian "Cogito"

If Maritain does not suggest that modern philosophy be given a place of honor in his proposed synthesis of human knowledge, it is not an oversight. One of his earliest controversial books was entitled *Antimoderne* (1922), and it resulted in his being labeled a reactionary thinker. Although it would be grossly inaccurate to make Maritain out a reactionary thinker, there is a persistent strain of prophetic warnings throughout his works that are directed at a characteristically modern trend in philosophy. It is the same philosophical problem that one finds at the beginning of *A Preface to Metaphysics,* where he argues against the moderns' prejudice against metaphysics. It is the same philosophical problem that underlies the argument in *Integral Humanism*. And it is the same issue that prompted Maritain to write in the old inflammatory style of *Antimoderne* in 1966, when he published *The Peasant of the Garonne*. Perhaps the most glaringly culpable instigators of modern intellectual errors, according to Maritain, are the trio who appear in the title of his 1925 book, *Three Reformers: Luther, Descartes, Rousseau*. Of these three, Descartes is naturally the one whom Maritain considered most pernicious for philosophy. The issue of Cartesian idealism, and all of its latter-day versions, as contrasted with Aristotelian-Thomist realism (here called "critical realism"), is the problem that Maritain sees as crucial to his epistemological argument, and he devotes much of the first part of *The Degrees of Knowledge* to an elaboration of the issue.

Maritain sees a long line of philosophical errors, beginning with Descartes and continuing in the thought of Kant, Hegel, and present-day phenomenologists. As different as these systems may be in some respects, the source of their various misconceptions is the same, namely the fatal Cartesian mistake of taking critique of knowledge (or epistemology) as the starting point of philosophy. The *cogito,* in turn, Descartes took as the starting point of epistemology. In other words, he ignored the *reflexive* (and, therefore, secondary) nature of critique. Because critique *is* reflexive, it must first consider the intellectual apprehension of the real. The starting point for critique, he says, rather than an awareness of the pure *cogito* of Cartesian idealism, must be an awareness of the metaphysical principle of identity that is behind the *cogito.* "Critique . . . implies the self-consciousness of the mind philosophically turning back upon its previous work of knowing" (DK, 75). In epistemology, in other words, the philosopher begins by assuming that what is, is. It is absurd for Descartes to propose to begin his grand philosophical method, says Maritain, by a systematic, universal doubt, for such a method entails "the negation of something about which we pretend not to know anything as yet (I mean the essential ordination of the intellect to being)" (DK, 78).

All these epistemological problems are intimately related to another aspect of what Maritain calls the "ferment of Cartesianism," the distinction between "thing" and "object." Perhaps the most concise and lucid statement of this distinction is the idea that "the way things exist in our thought, so as to be known, is not the same as the way they exist in themselves" (DK, 84). Things as they are presented to our intelligence are "objects" of thought, but they have a prior, and primary, existence in themselves as "things." They have an ontological value independent of our knowing faculty, a value that Maritain calls "premental . . . metalogical." Descartes and his heirs inaugurated a philosophical adherence to the primacy of object over thing. Hence, they are called idealists, whereas Aristotelian Thomists are properly called realists.

With these things in mind, it is possible for Maritain to express the essential difference between the Cartesian and Thomist versions of critique in the following terms: "The *cogitatum* of the first *cogito* is not *cogitatum*, but *ens*" (DK, 108). Because of this basic difference, the Cartesians consider Thomism a naive realism, "because, as far as they are concerned, naïveté is to start with an act of knowledge about things rather than with an act of knowledge about knowledge" (DK, 107).

Another distinction that is rendered meaningless by the idealist error is the one between the "possible real" (that which *can* have ontological content outside of and autonomous of the mind, even though it doesn't at the moment of its conception by the mind) and the "being of reason" (that which can exist only in the mind). For the critical realist, critique of knowledge is concerned primarily with the possible real, whereas the Cartesian idealist recognizes "the actual real as the only real" (DK, 92), and is thereby severely limited.

Finally, the idealist prejudice makes it impossible for a philosopher to understand the intentionality of knowledge, another concept that is vital in the Thomist scheme.

Above all, intentionality is a property of thought, a prerogative of its immateriality, whereby being in itself, posited "outside it," i.e., being which is fully independent of the act of thought, becomes a thing existing within it, set up for it and integrated into its own act through which, from that moment, they both exist in thought with a single, self-same supra-subjective existence. (DK, 103)

Thanks to the immateriality of thought, being can exist both outside the mind and within it. Its existence within the mind, however, has absolutely no effect upon its actual existence outside the mind. Knowledge modifies the knower by introducing into his intelligence what has its true existence outside him, but it does not in any way change the thing known. The ontological essence of the thing known remains intact throughout the process of being made present to the mind. In this context, Aquinas's definition of truth is especially clear: "*adequatio rei et intellectus,* adequation or conformity between intellect and thing" (DK, 80).

It is clear that Maritain feels no tenderness for idealism. Indeed, at one point he describes the idealist's relation to the world of critical realism as being "suspended [to it] like a parasite trying to suck its host into itself" (DK, 105). But he also identifies one important contribution of the Cartesian *cogito* to philosophy, that of bringing about a new critical, reflexive stage in the history of philosophy, a stage in which philosophy has become more aware of the spirituality of reason.

III *The Nature of Knowing*

Having thus traced a historical perspective of the philosophy of knowledge, Maritain next places within this context a summary of the Thomist theories on the nature of knowing. This he does, however, not without observing that modern philosophers have never elaborated a theory of knowing, for the simple reason that they have never been able to ask themselves the question, "What is knowledge?" The succeeding pages of *The Degrees of Knowledge,* then, give the altogether essential ideas upon which Maritain's epistemology is based.

First, the Thomist holds that there is a very close correlation between immateriality and knowledge. A being is a knowing being to the extent that it is immaterial. For to know is "to become a thing other than the self" (DK, 112), which, of course, is an apparent contradiction of the principle of identity. In order to understand that this mysterious union between the knower and the known (which constitutes knowledge) is not a contradiction of the principle of identity, we must admit the profound immateriality of knowledge. For, in addition to their existence in themselves as posited outside nothingness, the knower and the known must also have an "entirely tendential and immaterial existence" (DK, 114) through which the known is made present within the knower and the knower becomes the known.

Thus, knowing does not belong to Aristotle's categories of action or passion. It produces nothing. It is, instead, a perfectly immanent and vital quality, a superior mode of existence in which the knower participates. "Knowing is an active, immaterial superexistence whereby a subject not only exists with an existence limited to what that subject is as a thing enclosed within one genus—as a subject existing for itself—but with an unlimited existence in which by its own activity it is and becomes itself and other things" (DK, 113).

The most involved and difficult theories of Thomist epistemology concern the means by which the union of knower and known occurs. The Thomists called them *species:* "the whole world of intra-psychic immaterial forms that exist in the soul as vicars of the object" (DK, 115). The term for them that Maritain draws from the modern idiom is that of "presentative forms." An analysis of these intrapsychic forms reveals knowledge as a two part process within the intelligence. First, the knower becomes the known by means of the *species impressa,* or received presentative form, the form in which the known becomes immanent within the intelligence. Then the knower produces a *species expressa,* an elaborated or uttered presentative form, which it stores in its imagination or memory. So, the presentative forms *(species)* are pure likenesses of the object of thought by which it exists in the subject. They are the prerequisite conditions for and the means of knowledge, but they must not be mistaken for knowledge itself.

In this theory of the means of knowledge lies, in unusually lucid form, the essential difference between Maritain's critical realism and neo-Cartesian idealism. By a radical separation of "object" and "thing," Descartes reduced thought to a profoundly flawed, purely mental reproduction of reality, and the relation between reality and thought became quite nebulous. But in the Aristotelian-Thomist concept of knowledge, reality is immaterially present within the mind. And although there is a real distinction between the world of existence and the world of intelligibility, "it is by reintegrating the intelligible in the thing that exists . . . that the intellect completes its grasping of the real" (DK, 131).

IV   *Knowledge of Physical Reality*

Of the three degrees of abstraction in knowledge, the first—that of sensible nature—is the only domain that is properly subjected to two different knowledges. The second degree, the praeter-real, is a universe of knowledge ruled exclusively by mathematics. The third, or trans-sensible, realm of knowledge comes under the scrutiny of metaphysics alone. But there are two distinct knowledges that share the universe of the sensible real—the philosophy of nature and the experimental sciences. It is in this realm of knowledge that philosophy and modern science have conflicted most violently, and it is here, too, that it thus becomes especially important to Maritain to distinguish and unite, to lead science and philosophy toward a more fruitful, cooperative effort.

Maritain defines the philosophy of nature as "a knowledge whose object, present in all things of corporeal nature, is mobile being as such and the ontological principles which account for its mutability" (DK, 176). Like all other philosophies it employs an analyticosynthetic method, but it depends to a far greater degree on experience and sense verifications than on metaphysics.

Physicomathematical science, which shares the physical world with the philosophy of nature, is a knowledge of sensible reality that is translated into almost wholly quantitative symbols. It cannot seek out the nature itself of physical causes. Maritain calls it a "mythopoetical" knowledge of the sensible real, because its quantitative symbols are beings of reason that do not always necessarily bear a faithful relation to the actual real. Only by taking into consideration an exact doctrine of quantity supplied by the philosophy of nature may we understand the relation of these beings of reason to ontological reality.

Physical reality abounds with entitative riches that are irreducible to quantity. But, by reason of its materiality, and from the fact that it emanates from corporeal substance through the intermediary of quantity, this world of qualities is subjected intrinsically to quantitative determinations (and that is why it is accessible to our extrinsic and artificial mensurations). (DK, 142)

So one of the great discoveries of the thinkers of our century is the idea that an exact philosophical definition of quantity does not precisely correspond to scientific measurements of it. And here Maritain centers a discussion of what he considers the most significant direction that modern experimental science has taken, the theories of the New Physics. These new ideas originated in Einstein's theory of relativity, as opposed to Newtonian, or "classical" physics. They constitute a reaction against mechanism, determinism, and positivism as they were articulated in the nineteenth century. Speaking of the New Physics, Maritain observes that "once it had crossed the threshold of the atomic world, it discovered that mechanics cannot account for the movement of a particle in a manner completely determined at each instant. . . . So we see science obliged to abandon determinism precisely under the form in which determinism is 'scientific' " (DK, 150 - 51).

Maritain sees the New Physics as an effort to free physical knowledge from the excessive influence of mathematical concepts such as absoluteness. He observes that it also frees science from ontological philosophy, since it deepens our awareness of the fact that science makes no claim to knowledge of the intrinsic nature of things. He quotes A. S. Eddington's remark that: "The physicist now regards his own external world in a way which I can only describe as more mystical, though not less exact and practical" (DK, 174). Ironically, this new awareness has the dual effect of at once increasing physicomathematical science's autonomy and of improving the climate for effecting a constructive, cooperative relationship between the experimental sciences and the philosophy of nature.

Scientists, philosophers, and poets are all involved in fundamentally the same search for knowledge, according to Maritain. If he sometimes writes his philosophy in the soaring, lyrical style of a poet and yet sometimes wanders into dazzlingly intricate scientific reasonings, it is because he sees all knowledge as a unified whole. Maritain is, in this sense, one of those rare examples of the true humanist. People have always been unable to fit him neatly into a category, whether it be art, philosophy, or theology, precisely because the humanist perspective from which he has written is one that defies classification.

In general, the relation of the philosophy of nature to the experimental sciences is of a symbiotic nature so to speak. They are "two distinct but incomplete knowledges, subject to different controls, the one above all of the intelligible, the other above all of the observable, which complete each other as best they can" (DK, 178). Maritain is characteristically at home in pointing out the paradoxical nature of the relationship, which epitomizes the process of distinguishing in order to unite. The two disciplines need each other but must also remain separate. The consequences of ignoring the distinctions between the two are quite serious, as Maritain points out in the historical examples of Spinoza and Bergson, whose heresy he describes in the following passage: "May it never be forgotten what an error it would be to try to build a Philosophy of Nature, and *a fortiori* a metaphysics, on the theoretical conclusions of modern physics and its explanations of the world, taken as ontological foundations" (DK, 189).

Maritain applauds examples of scientists who have not been afraid to allow philosophical concepts—such as the activity of the spirit—to enter the realm of physical nature. But he also warns that the cooperation of science and philosophy is fraught with "dangerous liaisons." The heuristic value of philosophy to science is a valid part of the humanist's unification of knowledge, but its success depends greatly on maintaining "the essential distinctions between objective fields, which cannot be confused without injury to the mind" (DK, 196). Indeed, the progress of science in modern times, according to Maritain, coincides with clearer differentiation of ontological and empiriological knowledge and their respective roles in man's quest for truth.

V *Metaphysical Knowledge*

The substance of Maritain's metaphysics is treated in *A Preface to Metaphysics,* but there are some important supplementary elucidations on the subject in *The Degrees of Knowledge.* Maritain suggests, for example, that all men have an innate "intellectual perception of being" which constitutes our primordial metaphysical intuition. We are not conscious of such an intellectual power, although it underlies every act of the intelligence, until it is "disengaged for itself by the abstraction of the trans-sensible" (DK, 215). Once a man can lay aside from his mind all the sensible and particular aspects of reality that clothe its ontological essence, he can be aware of perceiving the primordial principle of intelligibility: metaphysical being. Then and only then can he abstract his natural metaphysical intuition from the sense-dominated aspects of the intelligence that cluster around it. And here again one enters the realm of *abstractio formalis,* which was considered earlier in this chapter.

The scope of metaphysical knowledge includes epistemology or critique—"the reflexive knowledge of the relation of thought to being"; ontology—"the knowledge of being as being"; and pneumatology and natural theology—"the knowledge of pure spirits and the knowledge of God according as these knowledges are accessible to reason alone" (DK, 218). It does not include theology or mystical knowledge.

Maritain further clarifies the distinction between the knowledge of the sensible real in (1) the philosophy of nature and (2) the empirical sciences. He calls the former dianoetic and the latter perinoetic. That is to say, in the philosophy of nature, the intellect attains essential reality directly, immediately, whereas the same reality is apprehended in perinoetic intellection only by means of signs that tend to hide its ontological intelligibility. Dianoetic intellection, then, is a "central" knowledge, whereas perinoetic knowledge is "radial," attaining the center only by beginning on the circumference and proceeding from the outside in.

The apprehension of metaphysical reality—which, of course, is to be clearly distinguished from sensible reality—is accomplished by a third kind of knowledge, which Maritain calls ananoetic intellection. Metaphysical knowledge is ananoetic in the sense of being specular knowledge, whereby the divine is apprehended as in a mirror, or by analogy. Thanks to the implicit universal analogy of being, the created gives a reflected image of the uncreated. The divine reality, unknowable directly by the human mind, is rendered present to the intellect in the form of its analogates. God, thus, is rationally intelligible to us only by analogy, and our knowledge of Him—the ananoetic or metaphysical degree of intellection—is anything but circumscriptive. He is not rendered subject to our intellectual faculties, as the subjects of other degrees of intellection. The human intellect cannot delimit His being. "Ananoetic intellection crosses the infinite abyss which separates it from everything; but the analogous concepts it uses avow at the same time their impotence to enclose or delimit the reality they then designate. They make God known only by kneeling before Him" (DK, 225).

At the end of the first part of *The Degrees of Knowledge,* Maritain approaches the limits of rational knowledge and anticipates the subject of the second half of his study, the degrees of suprarational knowledge. He talks about the areas in which the two realms are in closest proximity, about the "way of knowing and the way of non-knowing," about the fact that the highest truths of metaphysics can be apprehended in a speculative fashion but that mystical knowledge attains the same truths to a superior degree, since it involves the soul in an experiential knowledge of those truths. "All that is still to formulate theses . . . : it is not yet to have . . . passed on to a higher kind of wisdom, so long as these truths are known only and not experienced, so long as they are only spoken of, not lived" (DK, 237 - 38).

VI *Mysticism and Theology*

At the summit of the hierarchy of human knowledge, there is an interplay among three wisdoms. Metaphysical wisdom is the highest degree of rational knowledge, and although it has some connections with the suprarational wisdoms (theology and mysticism), it must remain clearly distinguished from them by the fact that it concerns knowledge of divine reality insofar as it is attainable to reason alone. At this level, God as first cause is apprehended analogically by the human intelligence as He is reflected by His effects, His creation.

Once the barrier between rational and suprarational knowledge is passed, the human intelligence finds itself in the realm of faith, where God is known more directly as experienced and revealed. However, since faith is a knowledge, as Saint Paul says, of things unseen, it is not to be confused with beatific vision, which is possible only after earthly life. For in beatific vision, the soul knows God "BY and IN His very essence . . . without the mediation of any creature or concept" (DK, 249).

Within the suprarational realm of faith, then, are the higher two of the "three wisdoms" earlier suggested by Maritain: theology and mysticism. They are superior to metaphysics and inferior to beatific vision on the ascending ladder of the degrees of knowledge. Mystical experience is the highest of the three human wisdoms, which Maritain, using St. John of the Cross as principal source, defines as "an *experimental knowledge of the deep things of God,* or *a suffering of divine things,* an experience which leads the soul through a series of states and transformations until within the very depths of itself it feels the touch of divinity and 'experiences the life of God' " (DK, 247—quote from St. John of the Cross, *Living Flame of Love*). Theology he defines as "the science of revealed mysteries . . . reason illumined by faith" (DK, 249). It is no longer analogical, as in metaphysics, but a direct, albeit incomplete, knowledge of that which is revealed. Theology, however, is still not the equal of mystical wisdom, for the latter is "no longer a question of merely learning, but rather of suffering divine things" (DK, 253). Mystical wisdom is a suprarational mode of knowledge for which there are two basic prerequisites: the readiness, or openness, of the soul to receive the gifts of understanding and wisdom, and the inspiration of the Holy Spirit, which is the moving power in the process.

The soul in a state of grace has a special connaturality with God, a "co-nascence," or co-birth, through which the indwelling of the Divine Persons makes possible an affective union with God that is not attainable by reason alone. "Thus, mystical wisdom realizes here below the promise, that is inscribed on the very nature of sanctifying grace, of coming to an experimental fruition of God" (DK, 263).

In the 1970s, one may well wonder how Maritain might have explored the Faustian aspect of epistemology. It seems safe to assume that he could have used this very context—the degrees of suprarational knowledge—to examine Satanic forms of knowledge, knowledge of evil spirits, mediums, astrology. It also seems safe to conclude that he would have considered these to be bogus forms of knowledge. The most intriguing aspect of the question is what implications he would have seen for the present-day fascination with what has come to be called "mysticism," that is, witchcraft, the occult, etc.

Maritain addresses himself to some specific problems in the relation of mystical and philosophical experience, attempting once again to draw clear distinctions between the proper roles of each. For example, he admits the existence of a kind of natural spirituality in man, but states that it can be set free only by inspiration from the supernatural realm. Similarly, all metaphysical inquiry is sparked to one degree or other by a mystical aspiration. "The desire—an inefficacious one—of knowing the first cause in its essence is like a secret fire in the heart of the metaphysician" (DK, 267). The metaphysician has a natural mystical desire, even though the object of his desire is unknown to him.

However, because of the all-important distinction between nature and grace, a natural mystical desire must not be confused, insists Maritain, with authentic mystical experience. An experimental knowledge of God is possible only in the order of sanctifying grace. The existence of non-Christian mystics who seem to have reached an authentic mystical experience is acknowledged by Maritain, and he makes no attempt to dismiss them as bogus forms of mystical knowledge, although he does express a degree of reservation in many cases. His explanation, both in *The Degrees of Knowledge* and later in *The Church of Christ,* is that these mystics belong invisibly to Christ's church. "The saints who visibly belong to the Church enable us to recognize their far-off brethren who do not know Her and yet belong to Her invisibly. . . . In this spiritual man *par excellence* (St. Paul) all genuinely mystical life finds its model and measure" (DK, 274 - 75).

Addressing another problem in the relation of mysticism and philosophy, Maritain asserts that the study of metaphysics does not of itself require mystical experience. There are examples of natural intuitions that seem to be grace-given: the sudden and inexplicable intuitive revelation of one's sovereignly individual being, for instance. But these "grace-given" experiences belong more properly to the realm of poetic intuition. "There are, we say, living relations within the soul's synergetic activity between mystical experience and philosophy; but they are there without any transfusion or blending of their natures" (DK, 280). Metaphysics does indeed give one a desire for mystical wisdom, and mystical experience can be a source of enlightenment for the philosophical intellect, but the realms of rational and suprarational knowledge remain quite distinct.

VII *Augustine and John of the Cross: A Thomist View*

An excellent example of the usefulness of Maritain's schematization of knowledge is the way he applies it to the problem of the age-old conflicts between Augustinians and Thomists. He acknowledges their implicit differences on some points but insists that the number of points of agreement between Augustine and Thomas Aquinas are virtually infinite. Their essential points of disagreement lie in their intellectual attitudes and systems, but their wisdoms are totally harmonious.

Maritain believes that one of the reasons for misunderstanding in this matter is the widespread tendency to reduce Augustine's work to a philosophical system. He holds that an "Augustinian" philosophy does not exist, and that no one, therefore, should expect one from St. Augustine's teachings. They were given in the order and light of the infused gift of wisdom, and Augustine spoke from that perspective. By contrast, Aquinas spoke in the order and from the perspective of the intellect, of theological science, of philosophy—"disciplines that proceed according to the mode of pure knowing" (DK, 292).

Thus, it becomes evident that Maritain's essential argument centers around the distinctions between the higher wisdoms. Mystical wisdom was the catalyst of Augustine's thought, whereas Saint Thomas worked in and through the lower wisdom of theology. The philosophical rigor that was lacking in St. Augustine's teachings was supplied by Saint Thomas, who, all the same, remained scrupulously faithful to Augustine's mystical wisdom. Descartes, Jansenius, and Luther are cited by Maritain as examples of the process of philosophical materialization that has deformed Augustine's thought in modern times. St. Thomas alone, he suggests, "was able to extract from Augustine, but with Aristotle's arms, not Augustine's, a science of theology and a science of Christian philosophy" (DK, 301). "If the essential values of St. Augustine's thought are considered in their integrity, it must be admitted, as we have explained, that the sole metaphysical systematization of that thought which remains *essentially* Augustinian is the Thomistic synthesis" (DK, 306; Maritain's italics.)

In reading Maritain, one often finds that he does not hesitate to give rather lengthy direct quotations when his argument is taken largely unchanged from one of his favorite sources: Aquinas, Aristotle, or the Scriptures, for example. Thus, it is no surprise to find that his chapter on St. John of the Cross in *The Degrees of Knowledge* includes almost as much of direct quotation as of his own thoughts. The properly philosophical element here is Maritain's comparison of the saint's mystical teachings to the Thomist philosophical and theological system. Again, he is intent upon demonstrating the unity of these two interpreters of the faith while distinguishing the degrees of knowledge from which they wrote.

St. John of the Cross, he explains, wrote in the practical order, whose function is to lead souls to perfection, whereas St. Thomas Aquinas wrote in the speculative order, whose function is to teach what perfection is. The former evokes, and leads one toward, an incommunicable form of knowledge; the latter, a communicable form. The apparent contradictions in their teachings are largely a matter of difference in vocabularies, which correspond to the respective degrees of knowledge out of which they arise.

Is it surprising that in the great Doctor of 'secret wisdom,' science also be disguised? Once more, if we expect to find in him speculative science, *with its own language*, we are foredoomed to misunderstand him. It would be no less naive to be surprised that St. Thomas does not speak the language of practical science and that the 'nights' do not appear in his vocabulary. (DK, 344, note; Maritain's italics)

Maritain gives a detailed summary of St. John's teachings on mystical experience. The doctrine of the void, the night of the senses, all the preparatory stages of the mystic's progress are described, and their relation to Thomist thought is set forth. The doctrine, however, which best illustrates how mystical experience belongs here at the highest point of the epistemological hierarchy is a striking theory concerning mystical union. It is taken from the *Summa Theologiae*.

Recalling the Thomist theory of the immateriality of knowledge, in which the knower becomes the known as other, Maritain states that mystical union is an analogously immaterial process. It is "to lose oneself in the other as self, to alienate myself in the reality of the other to the extent that he becomes more me than I am myself" (DK, 368 - 69). Thus, the literally "ecstatic" element of love is consummated in the spiritual marriage of the soul to God.

Indeed, mystical union is so radical a transformation, according to St. Thomas, that in this highest of all degrees of human knowledge, the soul engaged in its supernatural activity of love gives birth to a new being within itself. It is an "intentional being of love," which is distinct from its entitative being or its being of nature, and through which the spiritual marriage occurs.

At one point in his exposition of St. John's teachings, Maritain is brought to a restatement of the fundamental thrust of his epistemology: "There are in the world of the mind structural differentiations and a diversity of dimensions whose recognition is of the greatest importance. Serious misunderstandings can be avoided only by assigning to each type of thought its exact situation in this sort of transcendental topography" (DK, 315 - 16).

The exercise of each field of knowledge must be confined to its proper level on the hierarchical ladder of human knowledge. But the concomitant lesson of Maritain's epistemology is that we should distinguish the degrees of knowledge only to unite them in a harmonious, complementary relationship. Only by putting its own house in order in this way can philosophy hope to address itself effectively to the fragmented confusion of the present age. For the very root causes of the contemporary global crisis in culture lie in the failure of Western philosophy to preserve the eternal values of truth in the face of new existential situations.

CHAPTER 4

Philosophy of Nature

I N approaching Maritain's philosphy of nature, it is important
to realize that his voracious intellectual curiosity led him
throughout his life to study not only philosophy, art, and literature, but also the natural sciences. His writings display a surprising range of intellectual mastery. One of his first projects as a
writer, it may be recalled, was compiling an encyclopedic reference work on practical life. And during the same period, he
was deeply involved at Heidelberg with the work of the experimental biologist Hans Driesch, whose neovitalism had a lasting
influence on Maritain's thought. Even in the posthumously published *Approches sans entraves,* one finds profoundly searching
inquiries into highly technical scientific problems, and in such
contexts it is apparent that Maritain does not treat such problems
from what would be termed a layman's point of view. It is this
familiarity with the basic concepts of modern science that enables
him to delineate properly the boundaries between natural philosophy and science, while emphasizing the necessity of harmo-
nizing their complementary roles.

In discussing Maritain's epistemology it was said that he
defined philosophy of nature as "a knowledge whose object,
present in all things of corporeal nature, is mobile being as such
and the ontological principles which account for its mutability"
(DK, 176). In *Philosophy of Nature,* he elaborates on the implications of such a definition, more sharply defining the role and
nature of natural philosophy as compared to the experimental
sciences.

Philosophy of nature, in the Thomist sense, is the branch of
philosophy that deals with the same subject matter as the natural
sciences. It is a philosophical science, then, not just a philosophy
of science. It belongs properly to the speculative order of philosophy, but it is at the most humble level of speculative philosophy, since it depends for ultimate verifications on reference to

sense perceptions. Since its formal object is the sensible real as mutable, it shares the first degree of abstractive visualization with the sciences, and it is situated below the second and third degrees of abstraction, respectively: being as quantitative (the realm of mathematics) and being as being (metaphysics). The fact that it shares the realm of sensible being with the sciences is the primary source of the confusion with which philosophy of nature has been fraught throughout history. Maritain seeks in *Philosophy of Nature*[1] to clear up the major misconceptions and to account for the reasons they have arisen.

One of the major texts on this problem that Maritain wrote before *Philosophy of Nature* is found in *The Degrees of Knowledge*. And in *Philosophy of Nature,* as in the earlier epistemological study, he is concerned above all with distinguishing the degrees of knowledge in order to unite them. *Philosophia naturalis,* as Aristotle termed it, runs the constant risk of being absorbed by the experimental sciences on one hand and metaphysics on the other. *Philosophy of Nature* is largely a plea for the autonomy of natural philosophy, its "specificity as knowledge." The author thus devotes the first two chapters to a historical perspective on natural philosophy in Western culture. First, he discusses the strengths and weaknesses of the ancient philosophers' understanding of physical reality, and he then contrasts it with the generally positivist concept of physical reality in modern times. Finally, he concludes by selecting the most valuable contributions of each system of thought, which Thomist epistemology proposes to harmonize into a more thorough synthesis of the knowledge of physical reality.

The principle that must be kept in mind is the essential heterogeneity of the three degrees of abstractive visualization that share the speculative realm of philosophy. Maritain sums up this principle with the following formula: "Physical knowledge terminates in the sensible; mathematical knowledge terminates in the imaginable; metaphysical knowledge in the pure intelligible" (PN, 25). It is according to these different modes of abstractive visualization that the speculative degrees of knowledge are distinguished. But even more importantly for the matter at hand, the physical knowledge that Maritain says terminates in the sensible is composed of two specifically distinct disciplines: philosophy of nature and the sciences. The philosophy of nature is an ontological analysis of natural phenomena, whereas the

experimental sciences analyze the same phenomena empiriologi-
cally. "In one case [experimental sciences] the definition is sought
by means of possibilities of observation and measurement,
by effectuable physical operations; in the other, it is sought by
means of ontological characteristics, of elements that consitu a
nature or intelligible essence" (PN, 75).

I *Evolution of Philosophy of Nature*

Maritain observes that pre-Aristotelian philosophy—especially
as represented in Heraclitus and Plato—considered a reliable
knowledge of nature to be impossible, principally because of the
baffling aspect of physical reality that is called becoming, or
mutability. Because of this rejection of the knowledge of sensible
reality, Plato came up with a metaphysics that is based on logical
concepts, or beings of reason. According to Maritain, "Platonic
ideas . . . are essences which are separate from things, a state
of separation which exists only in the mind" (PN, 8). He asserts
that the great discovery of Aristotle was that knowledge of
sensible reality is, after all, possible, "not indeed insofar as
sensible nature is sense-perceived, but insofar as intelligible
elements and laws are vested in sense-perceived being" (PN, 10).
Aristotle, as Dante says, was "the master of those who know,"
and he was the first great champion of the philosophy of nature.
But in what sense was Aristotelian philosophy lacking in
knowledge of the sensible real, and why? Maritain quite readily
admits that the ancients were guilty of a very costly philosophical
error, what he calls "an error of intellectual precipitation" (PN,
33). Their faith in natural philosophy was excessive. They
expected it to supply explanations of phenomena in the physical
world. Relying solely on philosophy, they arrived at hasty and
often spurious theories of scientific problems such as the
explanations of rainbows, meteors, snow crystals, etc. In other
words, in the Aristotelian system, philosophy of nature usurped
the proper sphere of the experimental sciences. "To absorb all
the sciences of nature into the philosophy of nature was an error
in the speculative realm and we are much indebted on this point
to the work of modern times for a historic gain which the
Thomistic synthesis must always take into account" (PN, 35).
Whereas the ancients thus revered philosophy of nature at the
expense of the experimental sciences, the moderns have allowed

the growth of the latter to swallow up the philosophy of nature. One of the typical tragic modern errors is the radical mathematization of knowledge by Descartes. In the Cartesian system, a bogus philosophy of nature appears in a rigorously mechanistic form. "As a result, since science aims at giving a mathematical interpretation of sensible nature, it will be thought that science, —confused with the philosophy of nature—, must explain the whole of ontological reality by extension and movement" (PN, 43). One of the pernicious consequences of this kind of reasoning is that the whole Cartesian system of philosophy is built on a basically flawed pseudo-philosophy of nature. The various modern metaphysical theories, for example, which were so influenced by Descartes, were foredoomed from the outset by having originated in "a so-called philosophy of nature which was the mechanistic hypostasis of the physico-mathematical method" (PN, 44).

Maritain sees a direct line of development from Descartes to positivism. Descartes, he holds, was perfectly aware that spiritual and even organic life could not be fully explained in mechanistic terms. And so he erected not only an absolutely mechanistic system of knowledge of the corporeal world, but also and concomitantly, an absolutely spiritualist conception of the world of thought. Thence the infamous trap of Cartesian dualism. In the nineteenth century, this dualism was simply severed. The positivists chose to eliminate entirely the spiritualist half of the Cartesian system and to uphold a new purified science of phenomena, a science that would "keep itself undefiled, as from epistemological impurity, from every question and pretension about being, substance, cause, the 'why,' etc" (PN, 50 - 51). This positivistic purism, which is epitomized in the theories of Auguste Comte, sought to exclude all metaphysics and theology from its purview. And in so doing it set itself up as a counter-philosophy, thus doing violence to itself. For a strictly empiriological discipline can never successfully function in place of ontology in human thought.

Positivistic purism, admits Maritain, did indeed have healthy effects on the intellect. The asceticism that is required of science freed it from many excesses of imagination, anthropomorphism, and intuition. The deleterious effect toward which it tended, on the other hand, was to make knowledge into "a pure decomposition of the real, into a dust of mathematical beings of reason"

(PN, 53). And the most serious consequence, for Maritain, is that once there is no philosophy of nature, one cannot possibly have an authentic metaphysics. "Metaphysics itself is soundly constituted only by presupposing a philosophy of nature which it uses as its material basis" (PN, 122). It depends on philosophy of nature to preserve its contact with the sensible real, without which metaphysics becomes a sterile reflexive action of the intellect, not unlike the pure reflexive epistemology of the idealists described in Chapter 3.

II *Contemporary Renewals of Philosophy of Nature*

Although Maritain sees the trend of the experimental sciences between Galileo and the twentieth century as characteristically pointing toward positivism, he points to a number of his contemporaries as examples of reaction against the theories of Auguste Comte and company. Pierre Duhem demonstrated that positivistic purism, when pursued to its extreme, ultimately results in a pure mathematization of knowledge. This tendency, in turn, leaves room logically for an alternative interpretation of nature, one in which notions of quality are restored. Hence, the theories of Comte implicitly call for ontological analysis in order to complete themselves.

In the works of Emile Meyerson, Maritain points to the example of an epistemologist analyzing the functioning of the scientific intellect. Meyerson found the processes of scientific investigation to be "haunted by ontological and explanatory preoccupations" (PN, 62 - 63). In Meyerson's *De l'explication dans les sciences,*[2] Maritain finds an explicit confirmation of the Thomist teaching that science depends on philosophy. He quotes: "All science rests upon the unconspicuous . . . but nevertheless solid bed-rock of the belief in being that is independent of consciousness" (PN, 63). Duhem and Meyerson, along with Gaston Bachelard and the German phenomenologists, pave the way for a renewal of philosophy of nature. In biology, he cites Hans Driesch, Hans André, and Rémy Collin for their ontological perspectives on the science of the living organism. Lorentz, Poincaré, Einstein, Planck, Bohr, and others are illustrative of the movement in modern physics toward restoring "the sense of the ontological mystery of the material world" (PN, 152).

If Maritain is right in concluding that science today has begun to discover anew the value of philosophical knowledge of the sensible realm, it becomes doubly important that contemporary scientists and philosophers keep foremost in their minds clear distinctions between the functions of these two disciplines which share a common object. Maritain's interpretation of Pierre Duhem asserts that even the experimental sciences properly conceived as distinct from philosophy of nature cannot be thought of as devoid of ontological content. He thus rejects any purist conception of either science or philosophy of nature. Those two disciplines, like all the other "degrees of knowledge," are distinct. Yet they are not separate. Here again, the thrust of Maritain's work is an effort to distinguish in order to unite. As always, the guiding principle of Thomist philosophy that under-girds his theory is a vision of the integral unity of human knowledge.

How, then, do science and natural philosophy differ, and to what extent do they converge? First, they are not separate because they both share the same object, the sensible real inso-far as it is mutable. In Thomism's terminology, they do not differ generically. Their essential distinction lies in a *specific* difference in their methods of apprehending the sensible real: the empiriological and ontological approaches that were contrasted earlier in this chapter. Their modes of defining and concep-tualizing physical reality are so different that certain identical terms used in both disciplines may come to have altogether different meanings. But a more nearly complete analysis of physical reality requires a complementary relationship between the two. Maritain suggests the following analogy: The philosophy of nature is to experimental science as the soul is to the body. The sciences need philosophy of nature

as directive principles orienting thought and research, but not entering into the very structure of these sciences themselves. . . . But at the same time, science thus oriented by the philosophy of nature must keep itself from rising to the properly philosophical plane, since it must be held within the limits of empiriological analysis and of the empiriological vocabulary; that is to say, it must keep on resolving its concepts in the observable and not in intelligible being as such.   (PN, 111)

One of the most important problems implicit in suggesting a kind of symbiotic relationship between philosophy and science is the question of the role of scientific facts in philosophical reasoning. How should philosophy of nature regard scientific data? According to Maritain, the philosopher must avoid the errors of two extremes in this question. First, he must not reject scientific data, for they often present the philosopher with insights that allow him to find more satisfactory explanations of physical phenomena. But he must also resist the temptation to appropriate scientific data in the form of brute facts without interpreting them philosophically. It is imperative "that the philosopher use scientific facts only on the condition that he *treat* them philosophically, deliver them of the philosophical values with which they are pregnant, draw from them facts that have philosophical value" (PN, 146 - 47; Maritain's italics).

One branch of physical science in which Maritain outlines in more detail the structure of physical knowledge along the lines of the Thomist epistemological synthesis is biology. He suggests that biology lends itself to a division into three main parts: physicomathematical biology, typological biology, and philosophical biology. In the first kind of biological discipline, the scientist is concerned with physicochemical explanations of life, what Maritain calls "the material conditioning of life." Those scientists who engage in the search for a chemical formula for the secret of the living organism are the most extreme examples of the physicomathematical type of research, in which life is analyzed in terms of its nonliving components. The second division of biological knowledge is called typological or formally experimental biology. Here the scientist analyzes the living being as such and draws conclusions on the nature and functioning of the organism. The experimental biologist relies on philosophical considerations to orient his research, but he resolves his findings in terms of the observable. In other words, he uses the empiriological methodology and vocabulary, rather than the ontological. It is for the philosophical biologist, the philosopher of the organism, to arrive at ontological explanations of life. And he, in turn, must make philosophical interpretations of the scientific data put at his disposal by the other two kinds of biologists.

III   *New Applications of Philosophy of Nature*

The posthumously published *Approches sans entraves* provides an example of the role that Maritain envisioned for the Thomist philosopher of nature. In a long chapter that traces a preliminary sketch of a Thomist doctrine of evolution, he broaches various subjects of an extremely controversial nature. It is an intriguing prospect to imagine how far these issues might have been developed, had he not been already so near death.

Rejecting outright the Teilhardian doctrine of evolution, which sees the world as a progressive cosmic incarnation of Christ, Maritain predictably guides his reader back to a passage of Thomas Aquinas. In a careful reading of chapter 22, book III, of the *Summa Contra Gentiles,* he demonstrates that Aquinas offers the true basis of a philosophy of evolution. Teilhard, says Maritain, lacked the most important evolutionary concept, that of the change of being. "To him, everything was in everything, and what he, like many evolutionists not sufficiently versed in metaphysics, called evolution was no more than a 'disenvelopment.' "[3] According to the aforementioned text of Aquinas, on the other hand, there are actual substantial transformations in the evolution of human life.

Saint Thomas found in life a hierarchy, an ascending order in the perfection of forms according to which the substantial transformations occur. This hierarchy consists respectively of plant life, animal life, and human life, and there is an immanent upward tendenciality in these degrees of generation. Even in the development of the human foetus, Aquinas sees a reflection of the evolutionary pattern: There is first a vegetative phase, then a sensitive or animal stage, and finally an intellective stage. And it is only in this third stage that the immortal soul passes into the spiritual intellective plane.

In thus returning to a directly Thomist interpretation, Maritain takes issue with the majority of modern Catholic theologians, who hold that the intellective soul is infused in the embryo at the very moment of conception. Indeed, he faults those theologians for taking such a position not for ontological-philosophical reasons but out of dogmatic expediency. They embrace, he charges, an unsound philosophical theory in order to reinforce the church's teachings concerning abortions and the Immaculate Conception. But according to Maritain, these dogmas are in complete agreement with the Thomist concept of embryonic development. It is indeed a sin, he says, to kill an embryo that, although not yet fully endowed with an intellective soul, does possess a vegetative or sensitive soul with the virtuality of the intellective state. And the Virgin Mary was indeed miraculously preserved *in advance* from all sin by the future merits of the Son. Maritain's version of evolution is neither a bald appropriation of Darwinism nor a fuzzy-minded mysticism with only tenuous empiriological foundations. Instead, he carefully makes philosophical interpretations of modern scientific data on evolution and focuses on the points at which Saint Thomas's philosophy and the Holy Scriptures enlighten the subject. He obviously accepts the biblical account of creation, but not in the form of a ·scientific treatise. Genesis, he says, was not meant to convey scientific information but to instruct man concerning "the profoundest meaning of the real in God's sight."[4]

The immanent upward tendenciality described in the passage from Aquinas is a very important basic concept for the Thomist evolutionary doctrine. It is the driving force (Maritain calls it the "dynamism of nature") behind the natural processes of both embryonic development and evolution of the species. In animal procreation, it pushes embryonic development from the vegetative to the sensitive phase. In human generation, it does the same, but it is incapable alone to effectuate the passing of the human soul to the spiritual, intellective phase. For the creation of the intellective soul, God must intervene. Not repeatedly for each human being, but as a self-perpetuating effect of his original free act of creativity in breathing the breath of life into Adam. "The creative act is absolutely one in the unique, boundless Instant which is divine eternity. . . . For God it is the same thing to create Man and to create all men."[5]

The crux of Maritain's argument is a concern for balancing the dynamism of nature and God's absolutely free, gratuitous creativity. The role of the former cannot be allowed to usurp the latter, for that would amount to an excessively mechanistic theory. Of course, one must remember that Maritain acknowledges the dynamism of nature itself as a creation of God.

The thorniest problem Maritain considers in his discussion of evolution is a point of contradiction between science and philosophy. Scientists insist that the last and most advanced evolutionary state of homonoid primates, those from which man developed, could not have been animals. The Neanderthal period, for example, has left traces of a preculture and of tools that could not have been fashioned by any animal known to man today. Philosophy, on the other hand, holds that these same primates could not properly be called men because they lacked the human spiritual soul. It is the philosopher, not the scientist, who defines man, and the philosopher defines man as an animal endowed with an immortal, intellective, spiritual soul. And the difference between the animal soul and the human soul is so great that such an abyss cannot be bridged without God's supernatural intervention. "To think . . . that what current parlance calls animal intelligence . . . by gradually progressing can succeed in becoming [human] intellect is as absurd as thinking that an architect will one day reach the moon by building higher and higher towers."[6] There had to be a moment in which the gulf between animal and human was miraculously bridged.

In attempting to solve this impasse, Maritain offers a hypothesis. There must have been, he suggests, a group of animals at the apex of the primates' evolution that were so much like man that man was able to be born from them. These superdeveloped animals would have reached a psychic level above any other animals before or since while remaining at the subhuman or sensitive level of the soul's development strictly speaking. Their phylum would have been a more or less ephemeral one that would have vanished after the birth of man. Thus, they would represent the summit of evolutionary development made possible by the dynamism of nature alone—the appearance of an animal soul so highly developed physically and psychically that it called out, so to speak, for human intellect. But this ontological-metaphysical aspiration inherent in nature had to be completed by God's divinely free and gratuitous creativity. The enormous gulf between animal and human could never have been bridged alone by the dynamism of evolutionary development in nature. It took God's inscrutable freedom in act, the breathing of the breath of life into His new creation.

The above summary of certain teachings found in Maritain's last book offers illustrations of the concluding point in *Philosophy of Nature,* namely the constant change to which philosophy of nature is bound. Because it depends on ₋cience—which is characterized by a perpetual recasting of ideas and vocabulary— it is more subject to time than metaphysics. Philosophy of nature "must therefore submit to a certain law of aging and renewal" (PBN, 150). The substance of its teachings retains continuity, but it calls for renewals in concepts and terminology that will keep it abreast of new scientific discoveries. For these reasons, Maritain was concerned that Thomist philosophers reconsider ideas, such as evolution, in the light of modern scientific discoveries. That is why his "unfettered approaches" *(approches sans entraves)* to certain problems at the end of his career seemed quite iconoclastic.

CHAPTER 5

Social and Political Philosophy

IT is probably safe to say that the area in which Maritain's work has had its most widespread influence is the field of social and political philosophy. Certainly, he has published more books, taught more courses, and given more lectures in that realm of philosophical inquiry than in any other. And his contemporary readers have seen him most often as a thinker who has attempted to apply his faith to the most disturbing and controversial social and political crises of his time.

All this seems quite plausible, given the fact that the framework of the Thomist system of interpreting reality was already a fairly complete doctrine which Maritain inherited. His speculative philosophy owes more to Aquinas and the great commentators than does his practical philosophy. It is in this latter field that Maritain has come up with his most original insights. For here it is a matter of applying the Aristotelian-Thomist world view—the fundamental concepts of Maritain's metaphysics, philosophy of nature, and epistemology—to problems that are essentially of the moment. The test of a thinker's relevance to his own historical era is the degree to which he succeeds in bringing his speculative theories to bear on specific problems that are tied to that historical situation. In Maritain's case, the challenge of such a test confronted him inescapably at the time of the crisis of l'Action Française. Ever since that challenge, he has constantly addressed himself to the problems of social conflict, political theory, educational reform, and the place of culture in modern society. This last topic, including aesthetics and criticism, has been reserved for a separate chapter, since it will be considered in more detail.

"The Christian body has at such a time as ours two opposite dangers that it needs to avoid: the danger of seeking sanctity only in the desert, and the danger of forgetting the need of the desert for sanctity."[1] This statement, which appeared in one of the first books that grew out of Maritain's new social awareness in the 1930s, would be one of the most representative ones that could be chosen to illustrate the sometimes paradoxical combination of political liberalism and theological conservatism that has consistently inspired Maritain's stands on controversial issues. The main thrust of his political and social philosophy has been directed toward "ransoming the time," to coin a phrase (taken from St. Paul) that Maritain used for the title of his 1941 book.

I *Integral Humanism*

The single most important text among the many which Maritain has written in this area is *Humanisme Intégral,* originally published in 1936.[2] It is not without significance that the very first version of this book appeared in Spanish in 1935 with the title *Problemas Espirituales y Temporales de Una Nueva Cristiandad.* For Maritain's political thought had a truly profound influence on the whole Christian democratic movement in South America. Among the leaders of the movement who acknowledged a great debt to Maritain were Rafael Caldera of Venezuela, Eduardo Frei of Chile, and Amoroso Lima of Brazil. And *Integral Humanism* is the book by Maritain that Pope Paul VI cited in his encyclical *Populorum progressio* ("On the Development of Peoples").

The first English translation, entitled *True Humanism,* was unsatisfactory, as Maritain himself observed more than once, and he was understandably pleased when Joseph W. Evans undertook the task of writing a new English version entitled *Integral Humanism.*[3] Evans was Maritain's hand-picked translator during the last part of his career and is the director of the Jacques Maritain Center at the University of Notre Dame.

Integral Humanism is the charter that establishes the framework on which the Thomist responses to particular temporal issues—the finishing work in the construction of a Thomist political doctrine—are to be based. Other important books of sociopolitical doctrine include *Man and the State* (1951), *The Person and the Common Good* (1947), *The Rights of Man and Natural Law* (1942), *Du Régime temporel et de la liberté* or *Freedom in the Modern World* (1933), and *The Things That Are Not Caesar's* (1927). The last-mentioned work, originally published in French as *Primauté du spirituel* in 1927, was one of

the first important political writings of Maritain and grew
directly out of the papal censure of l'Action Française. It
announced a new openness on the author's part to the temporal
problems of his own age, a more mature attitude toward the
crisis of modern culture than he had manifested in such early
works as *Antimoderne*. Many other titles could be included
under the rubric of sociopolitical or moral philosophy, but these
are some of the most important ones.

The title *Integral Humanism* is a quintessential formula for
the fundamental concept on which all Maritain's moral philosophy is based. He is a humanist, and his concept of the nature
of man is the first tenet of his sociopolitical doctrine. But the
adjective "integral" qualifies Maritain's humanism in a vitally
important way. The Rousseauist connotations of unqualified
humanism give credence to what Maritain calls an absolute
humanist theology, the theology of natural goodness, in which
divine grace becomes assimilated into nature. Nothing could be
more remote from Maritain's own version of humanism.
"Existentially considered, one can therefore say that man is at
once a natural and a supernatural being" (IH, 10). Since man,
considered in his wholeness, is of a dual nature, humanism is an
essentially ambiguous term. Hence the necessity for the adjective
"integral."

"Integral humanism" is taken as synonymous with civilization
or culture. It is the force in history that "tends essentially to
render man more truly human" (IH, 2), and it serves all the
needs of the whole man, whether they be physical, emotional,
mental, or spiritual. This integralist understanding of man recurs
in all of Maritain's books, and it is repeatedly described in
contrast to the crisis in culture that has increasingly endangered
such a concept since the Renaissance. The progressive dissolution
of a culture based on medieval Christendom is recounted
through the historical periods that Maritain calls the classical
moment, the bourgeois moment, and the revolutionary moment.
Yet his discussion of medieval Christian civilization is not
plagued by a blind nostalgia for what is past, and he is careful to
point out the positive aspects of modern movements in culture.

II *Antihumanist Ideologies*

One of the most important accomplishments of Maritain's

sociopolitical writings is his analysis of the various modern political ideologies. One grave threat to humanism at the time when he first became involved in political philosophy was the growing menace of fascism. The tragic situations in Spain, Italy, and Germany in the 1930s were, in Maritain's view, a reflection of the lamentable decay in political philosophy during the classical, bourgeois, and revolutionary moments of history. The fundamental problem lay in the adulterated modern understanding of "sovereignty," a word that Maritain has clarified as meaning an absolute "supreme power *separate* and *transcendent* . . . and ruling the entire body politic *from above.*"[4] The concept of sovereignty, so defined, clearly can be assigned only to God. But modern thinkers have applied it erroneously to first the monarch, then the state, and finally, with Rousseau, to the body politic, or his mythical General Will. And since this General Will supposedly possessed unconditional autonomy, it excluded any smaller groups of citizens from the right to autonomy, thus creating a tyranny of enforced conformity that was a prototype for the fascist political order.

Maritain's condemnations of fascism have met virtually universal acclaim in the free world, but his evaluations of Communism have been much more controversial. In Chapter Two of *Integral Humanism* he offers an analysis of the Communist ideology that stands as a landmark of his political philosophy. From the very beginning he holds that Communism is nothing less than a *religion* for which dialectical materialism is the basic dogma, an essentially anti-Christian religion that claims man's absolute devotion and purports to reveal to him the meaning of life. Atheism, insists Maritain, is not required as a necessary consequence of such a doctrine; it is one of its principal constituent elements. It is a cornerstone of the entire Communist system.

Here Maritain pauses to give a brief but important treatment of the philosophical problem of atheism. "Atheism," he writes, "is *unlivable* in its metaphysical root, in its absolute radicalism. . . . For the will goes by nature to the good as such" (IH, 59; Maritain's italics). Citing the examples of Nietzsche and Dostoevski's Kirilov, he affirms that absolute atheism, when truly lived, can lead only to psychic dissolution. The peculiarly Russian Marxist form of atheism he interprets as a manifestation of resentment and retaliation against God for allowing evil in the world. In this, he most certainly was drawing on the traditions of Russian mysticism that he had come to know so deeply through his wife Raïssa and his friend Nicolai Berdiaev.

Jacques Maritain has taken a firm stand against Communism, but his is an eminently knowledgeable opposition. Even if his analysis didn't convey the degree to which he understands Marxism and its various modern incarnations, one would have only to remember his youthful enthusiasm for the cause of the proletariat in order to appreciate his deep understanding of the Communist ideology. He is careful to point out both the basic verities and the principal errors of Communism.

Marx, writes Maritain, has revealed to the world in a uniquely forceful way the alienation and dehumanization of social classes created by the capitalist system. This is the greatest truth of his work—a work that has indeed borrowed some important aspects of the Christian faith, according to Maritain. For example, Marx's messianic faith in the revolution as an eschatological elimination of man's enslavement to irrational forces is seen as an analogue to the Christian's expectation of the kingdom of God. But significantly the Marxist looks for the advent of the kingdom *in history,* an unrealizable ideal for the Christian.

The major accomplishments of Communism, according to Maritain, are the liquidation of the profit system and of the principle of the fecundity of money and the restoration of the dignity of work. Its most serious errors are a basic contempt for the human person and a persistent tendency toward bureaucratic despotism. In the final analysis, Communism is profoundly inhuman in that the price one pays for eliminating the dehumanizing inequities of capitalism is an abdication of the individual person's most profound spiritual aspirations for the benefit of collectivism.

From what has already been said, it is clear that Maritain's opposition to Communism is based on a metaphysical difference. He never even faintly implies that the only alternative to Communism is capitalism. Indeed, one of the most distasteful of all imaginable errors for him would be to tie Christendom to the capitalist economic system. "The temporal task of the Christian world," he reminds us, "is to work on earth for a socio-temporal realization of the Gospel truths" (IH, 42). But in modern times the Christian world has failed miserably in this mission. In fact, one of the most telling judgments on the Christian world is the fact that Communism—in adapting certain Christian elements such as the concept of communion and a spirit of faith and sacrifice—has taken over or usurped important areas of the apostolate for social justice.

III   *The Philosophical Foundations of Integral Humanism*

The Thomist finds it necessary to reject not only Communism, but also various nonatheist, non-Marxist social humanisms. Integral humanism calls instead for a more radical "substantial transformation." So radical, indeed, as to entail the "liquidation of bourgeois man," but not by means of violence. Through the power of grace and love, if a new Christian order will commit itself to a growing sociotemporal realization of the Gospel, implies Maritain, violence will certainly not be necessary for the elimination of bourgeois man. Here again, Maritain's vision of the new Christendom is clouded by an absence of specific means of implementation.

The philosophical foundations of the new Christendom, however, are clearly set forth, and close scrutiny reveals them to be quite sound. Maritain contrasts the Thomist's integral humanism with inhuman totalitarian systems and even with the Calvinist understanding of man as basically corrupt and totally devoid of dignity outside the election of divine grace. Whereas Maritain had referred to pure humanism as a doctrine of freedom without grace, he calls this antihumanist tendency in Calvinism a doctrine of grace without freedom. The creature (man), he insists, must be "truly respected *in* its connection with God and *because* receiving everything from Him; humanism, but theocentric humanism, rooted where man has his roots, integral humanism, humanism of the Incarnation" (IH, 72; Maritain's italics). And following up on the startling growth of modern man's self-consciousness since the Renaissance, Maritain emphasizes the need for a new "evangelical consciousness of self," a knowledge that sin both separates us from God *and* attracts His mercy.

One of the great accomplishments of a new Christendom, as Maritain sees it, would be a reversal of the modern trend toward polarizing the sacred and the profane. "The Christian world wounded by dualism (Descartes, Hegel, etc.) has obeyed two opposite rhythms, a religious rhythm for the time of the Church and of worship, a naturalist rhythm for the time of the world and of profane life" (IH, 78). For the Christian, the Gospel has transformed the rift created by pagan antiquity (and revived by Descartes and company) between the sacred and the profane. The Gospel by its very nature suffuses every aspect of the Christian's temporal activity. Hence, Paul's doctrine of the priesthood of all believers means, ultimately, that there is no such distinction as that of religious and secular vocations. "The man engaged in this secular or temporal order of activities can and must, like the man engaged in the sacred order, tend toward sanctity" (IH, 124).

IV   A Communal, Personalist, Peregrinal, and Pluralist Christendom

As to the major features of the temporal order envisioned by Maritain, it is important to note first that he carefully avoids the temptation of erecting a grand but impossible dreamworld. Thomas More, Fénelon, and others in the past were creators of utopian societies not susceptible of earthly realization. They have given us theories that have their own values as "beings of reason" but must not be seriously considered as blueprints for an actual social order. Maritain wants Christian philosophy to bypass the utopian stage and to proceed directly to a "concrete historical ideal . . . realizable not as something made, but as something on the way to being made" (IH, 128). This dynamic, on-going process of realization enables the Thomist political theorist to apply the eternally transcendent goal of the Gospel to the temporal order with all the necessary vicissitudes of successive historical moments. "A divine and hidden work is being pursued in history, and in each age of civilization . . . the Christian must work for a proportionate realization . . . of the Gospel exigencies and of Christian practical wisdom in the sociotemporal order" (IH, 126; Maritain's italics).

Here Maritain's philosophy of history enters the picture and clearly reveals its basic teaching. History, contrary to the doctrines of material determinism, is not characterized by an evolution toward a preordained fate. "One of the deepest trends of human history is precisely to escape more and more from fate" (IH, 131; Maritain's italics). Marx was wrong in concluding that one would have to escape from God in order to escape from fate.

Medieval Christendom, according to Maritain, was inspired by the concrete historical ideal of the Holy Empire, an ideal that was well suited to the medieval historical context, although certainly imperfect. The ideal, again concrete and realizable, that he suggests for a new modern Christendom is "the *holy freedom* of the creature whom grace unites to God" (IH, 163; Maritain's italics). The concept of freedom that characterized nineteenth century liberalism is altogether different. This anthropocentric and materialistic idea of freedom derives from Rousseau's spurious theology of natural goodness. On the other hand, the Aristotelian-Thomist version of freedom is based on the doctrine of integral humanism, in which due consideration is afforded to the spiritual aspirations of the human person.

Temporal society, for the integral humanist, is communal and personalist. That is, all men are ordered to a goal that may be called the temporal *common* good, but each individual *person's* spiritual worth is an essential factor that orients the common good. The end of temporal society is not to bring its citizens to sainthood, but to foster the growth of each person "to a level of material, intellectual, and moral life," and to enhance "the progressive conquest of his full life as a person and of his spiritual freedom" (IH, 134). The fundamental paradox of political life, then, is that it is concerned with accomplishing a common work to which individual human persons must be subordinate; yet the deepest aspiration of the person, "his eternal vocation . . . is superior to this common work and gives direction to it" (IH, 136).

While Maritain also points out the peregrinal nature of human temporal society, he insists that the Christian can never use this biblical doctrine as a pretext for the argument "that the present life is a vale of tears, that the Christian should resign himself to injustice or to the servile condition and misery of his brothers" (IH, 137). Medieval Christendom, says Maritain, was built on this communal, personalist, peregrinal understanding of political society, but it was a realization of biblical ideals of human society that was not only flawed but was also bound to a historical situation now remote, irrevocably lost. New alternative realizations are not only possible but essential to the good of mankind. Thus, the rejuvenated Thomist political philosophy offers a plan for ransoming the time by living out another Pauline distinction that is of utmost importance to Maritain—being *in* the world, but not *of* the world.

The new Christendom is envisioned as being necessarily plural-ist: "A Christian body politic in the conditions of modern times can only be a Christian body politic within whose walls un-believers and believers live together and share in the same temporal common good" (IH, 166). The unity of the new body politic would thus exist on a temporal plane and would be a minimal unity, by contrast to the maximal spiritual unity of medieval Christendom. But Maritain's suggestions for imple-menting a different juridical status for each non-Christian spiritual family in the body politic are rather vague. The goal of pluralism, at any rate, is clear: to maintain a vitally Christian orientation in the new political order while assuring justice and freedom for the non-Christian groups in that order. A pluralist economic structure would feature a degree of collectivization of ownership in the industrial sphere while renewing the principle of family economy and family ownership in the rural sector.

In line with this pluralist conception of the new political order, Maritain has offered quite an original idea for a political group that would play the formative role of leadership. This role, analogous to that of the Christian monarch in medieval times, would be played by "the most evolved politically and the most devoted part of the Christian laity" (IH, 168). The "civic fraternity," as he calls it, would be Christianly inspired; that is, it would embody the gifts of grace and charity, the infused virtues that come only from Christ, even though all the individuals of this fraternity would not necessarily acknowledge the Christian faith. By contrast with the Communist party, which plays the formative role in Communist countries, the civic fraternities would be founded on freedom and would be multiple. But they would also differ from democratic political parties as we now know them "by their essential structure and their moral discipline, as by the personal and spiritual effort which they would demand of their members" (IH, 171). Maritain finds a more apt analogy for the nature of the civic political fraternities by assigning them, in the secular domain, a relationship to the state that would be similar to the relationship, in the spiritual domain, of monastic orders to the church. The principal differ-ence would lie in the fact that the religious orders are principally monarchical by virtue of their rigid ecclesiastical hierarchies, whereas the civic fraternities would be principally democratic and would be independent of the state.

Once again, there are questionable points in Maritain's outline of the new Christian temporal order. His idea of how the executive branch of government would be changed, for example, seems somewhat wistful at best:

In a representative regime soundly conceived, in which the executive would be rendered sufficiently independent of the deliberative assemblies, the very possibility of using power to satisfy coalitions of interests and of cupidities would disappear. (IH, 171)

An executive branch . . . issuing from the people but in such a way as to be independent of the parties, would be free of any other preoccupation than that of the common good. (IH, 175)

A similarly unrealistic expectation raised by Maritain is his idea of the ownership of earthly goods. His basic principle is sound enough. He advocates not the abolition of private property, but a reformed policy of ownership intended to insure that "the use of goods individually appropriated must itself serve the common good of all" (IH, 184). It is in the industrial economic sphere that his plan seems to be weakened by impractical idealism. He suggests that in this sphere of the economy the new political order should insofar as possible replace the wage-earning concept by co-ownership, on the grounds that the dehumanization imposed by technology on the worker should be compensated by his participation in management. Thus, according to Maritain, the worker would have a better attitude toward his work, and increased productivity would be a by-product of the more humanized working atmosphere, owing to the new interest he would take in the success of the enterprise, in which he would now hold the advantage of coproprietorship.

While the feasibility of this solution seems doubtful, the principle behind it is well founded. "The problem is not to suppress private interest, but to purify it and to ennoble it; to hold it in social structures ordered to the common good, and also . . . to transform it interiorly by the sense of communion and fraternal friendship" (IH, 187).

Maritain carefully draws another distinction between depersonalized possession of things and the co-ownership of the means of work and the title of work, as they were understood in the medieval guilds. The new system of property, he holds, would foster pride in the excellence of craftsmanship and the dignity of work.

It is obvious by now that Maritain rejects not only fascism and communism, but also capitalism as a viable economic system in the new Christendom. This rejection, of course, should not be construed as a repudiation of the democratic political system, which all too often is associated with capitalism in the minds of Western capitalists. There is no guilt by association; on the contrary, although Maritain praises the medieval Christian monarchy almost as much as modern democracy, his plan for a new political order can be accurately called a Christianly inspired humanist democracy. But he remains firm in calling for the elimination of the capitalist economic system as a prerequisite to a Christian humanist state.

The new Christendom demands "a radical change not only in the material but also in the moral structure and in the spiritual principles of the economy" (IH, 190 - 91). The measure of all things in the capitalist economy is bound to antihumanist pre-occupations: productivity, technology, money. The only logical measure of all things for a humanist culture would be man. So that in the economic sphere, Maritain's integral humanism calls for a socialist redistribution of wealth.

To contemporary affluent America, this kind of talk may seem rash, even heretical. It is not easy to accept. But the wisdom of Maritain's Thomism may eventually prove prophetic. For Maritain already understood when he wrote *Humanisme Intégral* in 1936 what Americans have learned since then in the context, for example, of the civil rights movement. One cannot expect a political system to remake all men into molds of Christian charity. But, on the other hand, one must ask of the political order what it *can* do, namely to safeguard justice and equality by creating laws that are inspired by the Gospel exigencies and that naturally orient human energies toward the realization of those exigencies.

Modern civilization is a wornout garment. One cannot sew new pieces on it. It requires a total and, I may say, substantial recasting, a transvaluation of cultural principles: since it is a question of arriving at a vital primacy of quality over quantity, of work over money, of the human over the technological, of wisdom over science, of the common service of human persons over the individual covetousness of unlimited enrichment or the State's covetousness of unlimited power. (IH, 207)

V *Politics and Ethics*

What is the place of ethics in the Thomist political theory? Maritain, had he been confronted with this question, undoubtedly would have rephrased it to show that "political science constitutes a special branch of moral science . . . that which concerns specifically the good of men assembled in political society" (IH, 216). Ethics, then, undergirds politics and informs it with a moral orientation more or less consonant with its own concerns. This is not to say that a good ethics will necessarily produce a good political philosophy, for "it does not suffice to be just to be a good politician, but justice is a *necessary* condition of every good politics as such" (IH, 217; Maritain's italics).

Regarding the theory that the ends justify the means in the political sphere, Maritain's position is uncompromising. Politics concerns the common good of society, which is necessarily of a moral nature, and intrinsically evil means are essentially incompatible with it. Machiavelli systematized certain universal tendencies of human action, and in the political domain he made them into a form of art. The Machiavellian theory of *The Prince* is what Maritain calls "the technical rationalization of political life" (MS, 56), as opposed to "the moral rationalization of political life" (MS, 58), which can be accomplished only by a democracy suffused with the Gospel inspiration. Machiavelli's elimination of morality from politics is, for the Thomist, so pernicious as to lead ultimately to the most inhuman of political systems.

The rules of ethics can never be traced out in advance, since they depend on the contingencies of temporal existence. Thus, the politician is called to deal not with abstract essences but with the concrete world of existence. He will find it necessary to be able to choose wisely the lesser evil and "to tolerate evils whose interdiction would bring with it greater evils" (IH, 218). He must not be crippled by a pharisaic fear of soiling his hands in the political struggles of fallen man. He must not hesitate to judge of the moral quality of acts and to denounce injustices; yet he must remember that it is God's responsibility alone to judge the doer of those acts. For Christ, observes Maritain, was not only the great enemy of sin but the great friend of sinners.

VI *The Church and Political Society*

The proper relationship of the church and the political order is a problem that concerned Maritain throughout his career. It strikes at the very heart of his most persistent philosophical theme, the necessity for a supratemporal source of guiding philosophical principles and the application of these principles to pressing human political and social needs. The principle that forms the basis of his whole response to this question is what he has called "the primacy of the spiritual." This phrase, whose French equivalent was the original title of *The Things That Are Not Caesar's,* summarizes the belief that the temporal common good of man, although it is the supreme object of political life, is inspired from above by the spiritual aspirations of the human person. "Even in the natural order, the common good of the body politic implies an intrinsic though indirect ordination to something which transcends it. . . . To ignore these truths is to sin simultaneously against both the human person and the political common good" (MS, 149).

In the light of this basic truth, Maritain states three laws of the proper relation of church and state. The first of these laws is the freedom of the church. The doctrine of the church as the mystic body of Christ is developed in Thomist thought to mean that the church is an eternal person, to be clearly distinguished from her personnel. This rather intricate doctrine, which was earlier outlined by the Thomist writer Charles Journet, is delineated at length in Maritain's *On the Church of Christ* (1970). Because of this conception of the church, Maritain sees the church's freedom as a necessary aspect of the independence of the Incarnate Word, of God Himself. Second, the mystic body of Christ is superior to the body politic or to the state. For the State is "under the command of no superior authority in its own order. But the order of eternal life is superior in itself to the order of temporal life" (MS, 153). Maritain also points out the important fact that since the Kingdom of God is not of this world but spiritual, it should not be regarded as a threat to temporal governments. The third law stated by Maritain is that of the necessity for cooperation between church and state. Man unites the spiritual and temporal, and an absolute separation of church and state would cut him in half. He has constant needs that can be met only by a harmonious cooperative functioning of church and state.

The superiority of the church in no way suggests that she express her authority by dictating political policies to the civil powers. It is manifested instead in the spiritual enlightenment of citizens whose free participation in government in the political sphere of their lives will have a determining influence on such policies. The birth of a Christianly inspired temporal order depends upon a radical Christian renewal of society, upon the ability of Christians "as free men speaking to free men, to revive in the people the often unconscious Christian feelings and moral structures embodied in the history of the nations born out of old Christendom" (MS, 167).

For Maritain, Christian political action is not the responsibility of the church but of laymen working in the temporal sphere. The transformation of the temporal order is the mission of lay Christians exercising their political freedoms and responsibilities. The role of the church must be to create the mind of Christ in its members, to prepare them for that temporal mission. Commitment to a new Christendom demands political action at long range without ignoring the needs of the present. It will require patience, foresight, and an ability to effect progressively successful applications of the Gospel in the political and social realm.

It is altogether normal that there should be great diversity of political and social thought among people of the same faith. Christians who are united spiritually in the love of Christ will inevitably find themselves differing over the most desirable means of attaining the common good. But the action of a Christian in the temporal plane can never be entirely separated from his spiritual allegiances.

What you do, says St. Paul, do in the name and in the power of Christ. If grace regenerates us, if it makes each of us a 'new man,' is it in order that we should make a bargain with the 'old man' who in the temporal will serve Mammon? . . . Action is an epiphany of being. If grace takes hold of us and remakes us in the depth of our being, it is so that our whole action should feel its effects and be illuminated by it. (IH, 293)

The state, by the same token, has its own responsibilities toward the spiritual community. Strangely enough, the most important duty the state performs for the church is to serve effectively the temporal common good, for the maintenance of a just political order contributes to the well-being of the church and the fulfillment of her mission. Next, the state is required to insure "to the Church her full liberty and the free exercise of her spiritual mission" (MS, 177). Furthermore, it is essential to the survival of the democratic charter—not simply useful to the church's mission—that the state make frequent reference to the fact that the democratic political system is inspired by, and grounded in, belief in God's rule in human society. Thus, the state needs to practice the public acknowledgment of the existence of God.

There are numerous additional examples that Maritain gives of more particular forms of mutual service performed by the church and the state. But the essential feature of his analysis of their relationship is that their natures and functions should be sharply distinguished, while the need for their actual cooperation must be emphasized. "The cause of freedom and the cause of the Church are one in the defense of man" (MS, 187).

VII   Catholic Political Action: The Catholic Press

Jacques Maritain's involvement in journalism in the 1920s and 1930s is a revealing aspect of his work in relation to his conception of Christian political action. His collaboration in the periodicals *Sept* and *Esprit* was so instrumental that both grew to represent his own sociopolitical philosophy and its implications for the many controversies of that troubled time. Indeed, the delicate nature of certain issues eventually led to an unofficial censure by ecclesiastical authorities. In an appendix to *Humanisme Intégral* entitled "The Structure of Action," Maritain republished a careful analysis, which had first appeared in *Sept,* of the problem of the Catholic press. Here he argues that there is not only a spiritual plane in which a Christian may act as a Christian per se and a temporal plane in which he may act as a man who, though Christianly inspired, nevertheless does not represent the church in his action, but there is a third plane, an intermediate realm, "a zone of truths connected with the revealed truths of which the Church has the deposit, and which direct from above the temporal thought and activity of the Christian" (IH, 296). Papal encyclicals, for example, have elaborated a kind of Christian sociopolitical wisdom. It remains speculative enough to provide theological principles from which more concrete sociopolitical doctrines may be deduced. On this third plane, when the Christian addresses issues concerning marriage, education, etc., he "acts and appears before men *as a Christian as such,* and to this extent he engages the Church" (IH, 297; Maritain's italics).

Here one is confronted with the central problem of the Catholic press. For by extending these important distinctions, one finds that "to speak as a Catholic having a certain temporal position and to speak in the name of Catholicism are two very different things" (IH, 305). To pronounce publicly one's own stand on a controversial issue, one must clearly indicate whether he is speaking "as a Catholic as such," or as an individual who also happens to be a Catholic. It is an error of grave consequence to allow this distinction to be obscured or confused, because it threatens to compromise the church by binding her to a particular sociopolitical interest or party.

Thus, Maritain suggests that the Church should welcome and encourage the creation of religious periodicals while insisting on a clear distinction of the two types: those that are "specifically Catholic and religious, and as a result Catholic *by denomination,*" and those that are "specifically political or 'cultural' . . . but Catholic *in inspiration* only" (IH, 305; Maritain's italics). The first type of periodical pertains to Catholic action, the creation of the mind of Christ in the people, the conveying of a speculative Christian sociopolitical wisdom inspired directly by the Gospel. The second, once again, does not engage the church and is primarily concerned with a temporal task, not with the apostolate. Maritain's description of periodicals in this second category clearly includes such journals as *Esprit* and *Sept:* "They have adopted not only a political and social philosophy, but a well-defined concrete political and social line—not only in function of religious interests or of the good of the Church, but also in function of the temporal and terrestrial good of the body politic and of civilization" (IH, 307). The article is an excellent example of Maritain's own personal form of Catholic journalism, Christianly inspired, but not written as a Catholic speaking for the church.

VIII *Human Rights*

The Thomist philosophy of human rights reorients one's perspective on how laws and rights are derived from natural law. With his global awareness and a desire for international cooperation, Maritain points to the U. N.'s International Declaration of Rights (1948) as an example of the possibility of bringing many diverse cultures together and agreeing on a statement of basic human rights without compromising their conflicting philosophies or faiths. It is indicative of the global scope of Maritain's philosophy that he was asked to address the second International Congress of UNESCO on this subject in Mexico City in 1947. In his remarks he observed that a universal statement of human rights is possible on the condition that the reasons for including each right not be discussed. On the practical plane, certain basic rights can be acknowledged by all, but for very different reasons. Great disputes would arise from a discussion in the speculative order of the rational foundations of those rights. He further stated that he firmly believed his own philosophical basis for determining human rights, grounded in the Christian faith, was the only true one and that it is indeed important to know which faith is the true one. But the least that can be done toward international cooperation and understanding, he continued, is to agree on such a practical statement of basic human rights.

According to Maritain, there exists, in addition to a list of universally acceptable rights, a universal concept of natural law. He is careful to dispel from such a notion the philosophical errors that the enlightenment attached to it. The eighteenth century thinkers saw natural law as a written code of *a priori* rules for human conduct. In actuality, they had unconsciously come to a very arbitrary determination of such rules, and "this philosophy of rights ended up, after Rousseau and Kant, by treating the individual as a god and making all the rights ascribed to him the absolute and unlimited rights of a god" (MS, 83).

In the Aristotelian-Thomist concept of natural law, Maritain sees natural law reflected in the analogy of any work of human art. "Any kind of thing produced by human industry has . . . its own natural law, that is, the *normality of its functioning,* the proper way in which, by reason of its specific construction, it demands to be put into action, it 'should' be used" (MS, 86; Maritain's italics). By extension, then, man has his own "normality of functioning," which carries a moral aspect because he may in his freedom choose to conform to this "ideal order relating to human actions" or to transgress that order. It is important to distinguish this ideal order from a kind of preordained essence, as in the system of Leibnitz, that would decree in advance the proper regulation of each particular situation of human conduct.

Natural law is apprehended not in rational knowledge but in knowledge by inclination, knowledge by connaturality. And the most authentic example of progress in human history is the progress of moral conscience, by which man has come to an increasing inclination of the mind and heart toward the proper functioning of man.

The most dangerous implication of modern philosophies of human rights is their tendency to emphasize the rights of the people without proper concern for their concomitant obligations. At least, such was the tendency of theorists in the Enlightenment, who have so deeply influenced modern political thought. Maritain shows that the Thomist philosophy maintains a healthy balance between these two elements of natural law. He even calls attention to the distinction between possession and exercise of inalienable rights. Such basic human rights are possessed absolutely by all people, but individuals may, through criminal forfeiture of certain rights, be deprived of the opportunity to exercise those rights, even though they still possess them. Similarly, it is readily evident to students of history that in times of crisis and transition, new rights come into conflict with old ones. In such cases, it becomes necessary to restrict some rights, if only temporarily, in order to assure others. The most complicated problem of human rights then arises, namely, determining the degree of such restrictions and "the scale of values that governs the exercise and the concrete organization of these various rights" (MS, 106). Thus, as one moves from the fundamental rights of man into the realm of specific rights, which sometimes evolve and often conflict, one finds that the larger sociopolitical philosophy that one espouses will dictate differing ways of applying basic rights to individual economic and social contexts.

Whenever rights begin to conflict, there is a potential for a crisis of authority. Political authority comes under great pressure because it is expected to resolve the conflict equitably. And in recent political history, it has become increasingly apparent in democratic states that those groups who feel that their rights have been ignored or insufficiently recognized will resort to means of protest that will pose a challenge to authority. A thoroughgoing analysis of authority such as the one offered by Maritain is instructive and can be readily applied to political crises like those that have arisen in the recent past in the United States.

"Whatever the régime of political life may be, authority—that is, the right to direct and command—derives from the people, but has its primary source in the Author of nature" (MS, 127). The people have a natural right to govern themselves, and the political entity in which they invest the governing authority must act as the vicar of the people. The notion of vicariousness, as stated by Maritain, clarifies the relationship of the governing authority and the people. Again, sovereignty is the prerogative of neither. The president, or leader of the state, is not the image of God, as in the system of divine right. He is the image of the people, because his authority derives from the people. He leads the body politic, with their common good as supreme guide. But his authority, even though it is not permanent, is real. He has the right to command, and be obeyed, and his decisions must conform to the demands of his own political and ethical conscience, even when such decisions are not popular. Indeed, a great ruler or leader may at times attract great disfavor by taking actions that, although unpopular at the moment, eventually prove that he was acting according to a hidden higher will of the people. This is the ideal situation described by Maritain in *Man and the State:* "The happiest circumstance for the body politic obtains when the top men in the state are at the same time genuine prophets of the people" (MS, 140).

One of the striking ironies of Maritain's political thought is the resemblance between his descriptions of the ideal ruler and of the proper role of dissenting minorities, which he terms "prophetic shock-minorities." He asserts the importance of the latter even in normal times, but especially in times of crisis and renewal. For as in the relationship between leader and people, the shock minorities are leavening agents that awaken the people to a higher will. They give the lie to the tyranny of the majority, which develops from time to time because, for the most part, the people prefer to accept the status quo. The awakening is usually painful, and in the heat of the moment it is often difficult to determine whether the prophetic shock minorities are in the right. Samuel Adams, Gandhi, and Martin Luther King would have been opposed by the tyrannous majority in their revolution-

ary awakenings, but the test of time proved their minority movements to be truly prophetic. "The question is: are the people to
be *awakened* or to be *used?* To be awakened like men or to be
whipped and driven like cattle?" (MS, 142; Maritain's italics).
The perilous step that the shock minority must always take is the
one by which it claims to represent the hidden higher will of the
people. And the leaders of such groups must always realize that
Rousseau was wrong in wanting to force the people to be free.

IX   *World Government*

As one might well expect, the architect of a new Christendom
is also a proponent of world government. It simply seems unrealistic to Maritain to allow the modern world to become more and
more divided by narrow-minded nationalism in the face of its
growing economic unity, which is an inevitable trend of history.
As long as each individual nation allows its foreign policy to be
dictated by the *raison d'état,* there is no hope for peace. A
lasting peace can only reign when the basic causes of war have
been eliminated, and the primary cause of war is anarchy, or, in
the words of Mortimer Adler, "the condition of those who try to
live together without government" (quoted in MS, 196). Hence,
world government is necessary in order to insure world peace.
States must finally surrender their spurious claims to sovereignty.
The greatest source of confusion over the debate on world
government, according to Maritain, is the tendency on the part
of too many theorists to propose a purely governmental solution
to the problem, one that exclusively concerns the state. Maritain
holds that the most fundamental and most important political
reality is the body politic, rather than the state or the government. Therefore, the whole argument should center on the
organization of the world's political society—what Maritain calls
a "fully political" theory of world government. A merely
governmental idea of world government would lead to the creation of a vast superstate, which is no more than the age-old
dream of universal empire.
Far from accepting the superstate notion, Maritain proposes
instead a world government that would preserve the essential
identity and autonomy of individual nations in a federal system
not unlike the union of individual states in the U.S.A. But his
realism keeps him from suggesting immediate implementation of

such a plan. As in his blueprint for a new Christendom, Maritain charts out the gradual transformation of world political society beginning at a grassroots level and progressing upward. And he also avoids leaving his reader with a sense of disappointment and ineffectuality by suggesting an immediately realizable innovation that could prepare the way for a more permanent world political organization. This first step toward world government is what Maritain calls a world advisory council. He envisions it as an entity totally separate and independent from the United Nations which would be made up of members from various nations who would give up their nationalities in order to act with the utmost impartiality. They would have no military or judicial or legislative power, but would depend totally on the support of member nations. In this manner they would offer what Maritain considers a highly instrumental element in progressing toward world political organization, namely, the mobilization of world public opinion. "They would be simply free to tell the governments and the nations what they held to be just" (MS, 214).

The sociopolitical thought of Maritain is another example— and probably the most important one—of how this philosopher has returned to the writings of his master, Thomas Aquinas, and sifted them at a deeply personal level of insight in order to bring a long-forgotten perspective to the most trying problems of the modern age. His most earnest wish in writing on modern political problems was that Thomist truths might be resurrected in a whole new movement of political theory that would save the precious legacy of the past without its wornout trappings. He pointed out in *Reflections on America* that his given name Jacques means hope. Hope—the second of the theological virtues—is a hallmark of his political theory, for Maritain holds out the hope of a new political order in the spirit of the Western heritage at its best.

X   *The Example of America*

As observed above, Maritain's decision to return to the United States in 1948 after his term as French Ambassador to the Vatican had great significance in his career. He was choosing to make himself a presence and an influence on American society and a spokesman for American Catholic intellectuals. The great number of books that he published in English during the ensuing period attests to his importance in this country. And one of the reasons for that decision, it may be surmised, was the compatibility that he found between the American political system at its best and his own notion of a new Christian humanist political order. In fact, he stated in *Reflections on America* that *Integral Humanism* "appears to me now as a book which had, so to speak, an affinity with the American climate by anticipation."[5]

After the outbreak of World War II, Jacques Maritain lived more in the United States than in France, and he soon came to love this country very deeply. The book *Reflections on America,* which grew out of a seminar series he gave at the University of Chicago in 1956, is an example of how his political philosophy can be applied to a concrete case in point. No really good philosopher has a blind passion for a country, and Maritain's love for America does not preclude his pointing out the major problems inherent in our culture. He briefly examines the race question, for example, and has great praise for Martin Luther King's use of nonviolence. He sees the American obsession with sex as an anti-Puritan overreaction that must be outgrown. And he stresses the danger of the illusion that marriage is no more than the consummation of romantic love. The proper relation between man and woman he regards as an even more serious question than relations between labor and management or even between the races.

American intellectual modesty, for Maritain, is both admirable and lamentable. It fosters a sound experiential approach to practical matters, but it also runs the risk of philosophical empiricism and a "general and systematic fear of ideas." Americans must not allow this latter tendency in their natural intellectual modesty to hinder the articulation of a sound, explicit philosophy. The growth of such a philosophy, Maritain believes, would give Americans an awareness of the fact that they have already gone beyond both capitalism and socialism. Americans are not obliged to accept the ideological battle with the Communists on the latter's terms: that is, Communism versus capitalism. They must realize that the battle against Communism is a battle against the past, not the future, and that they are not forced by it to defend the capitalist economic system, but the democratic political system.

The importance of the United States as a model of political theory is summarized by Maritain in what he calls the principal "American lessons in political philosophy." Contrary to other countries, whose existence as bodies politic originated in wars, conquests, or some other form of constraint, "the American body politic is the only one which was fully and explicitly born of freedom, of the free determination of men to live together and work together at a common task" (REF, 168). Further, Maritain considers the American system to be the "best conceived and most efficient" of all democracies in existence, and he pays particular tribute to the Supreme Court, which he calls "one of the great political achievements of modern times."

Finally, Maritain outlines specific examples of the way in which he regards the American system as especially compatible with his proposals for a new Christendom. American society, he observes, is classless in the basic sense of lacking rigid hereditary social classes. The socioeconomic mobility of the American system is a first step toward integral humanism. He also admires the fundamental pluralism of American society, especially religious pluralism, which, of course, was one of the most important ingredients of American civilization from its birth. In a new Christendom, Maritain envisions a relation of government and religion not unlike the American ideal. The state cannot favor any particular denomination but must acknowledge the necessity for the continued inspiration of Christian reason.

Quoting the words of Jefferson, Lincoln, and other great architects of American democracy, Maritain concludes that nowhere are the conditions more conducive for a new political order based on Christian-inspired democracy than in the United States. "If a new Christian civilization, a new Christendom is ever to come about in human history, it is on American soil that it will find its starting point" (REF, 188).

CHAPTER 6

Philosophy of Education

MARITAIN spent most of his life in the academic community. He taught philosophy at many colleges and universities, and he lectured at campuses throughout the United States. Although, oddly enough, he claimed that teaching was primarily a financial necessity for him most of his life and that he was first a philosopher and writer, still his great personal charm, his incisive mind, and his intellectual courtesy made him a respected and valued teacher. His concern for the modern crisis in philosophy quite naturally led him to espouse a philosophy of education that would attempt to counteract the many influences exerted in that field by idealist and materialist philosophies. During his years in the United States, he met several important educators whose ideas were compatible with his own. Among acquaintances such as Robert Hutchins and John U. Nef, Maritain shared a mutual exchange of ideas, and the writings of Whitehead and Cardinal Newman also interested him. Yet with each of these men Maritain differed in certain significant respects, and beyond question the most important basic sources of his philosophy of education were Aristotle and Aquinas.

When Maritain gave the Dwight H. Terry Lectures at Yale University in 1943, his topic was "Education at the Crossroads," a title that he kept for the publication of the lectures in book form.[1] The critical state of education, as Maritain saw it in 1943, has not greatly changed since that time, and the problems he then saw are, for the most part, still all too real for contemporary educators. He aimed some of his reflections at the peculiar problems imposed by the postwar years he saw ahead, but his perspective on the more fundamental crisis that we still face is what the present chapter will consider.

I *Defining the Liberal Education*

The most difficult problems in education, both in 1943 and at the present, are outgrowths of two basic errors. The first is the whole mentality that favors the supremacy of means over ends. "The means are not bad. . . . The misfortune is precisely that they are so good that we lose sight of the end" (EC, 3). Once there is a loss of direction, a lack of a clear sense of purpose in education, the whole enterprise is doomed. The second error at the root of these problems is the confusion over the proper end of education. And, for Maritain, since the end of education is to become more fully human, redefining that end necessarily entails a discussion of the question, "What is man?" It is quite obvious that Maritain rigorously bases his educational doctrine on his speculative philosophy, his metaphysics and epistemology. It is only to be expected, he observes, that an empiricist, for example, should have a philosophy of education drastically different from that of a Thomist.

Maritain answers that fundamental question by drawing on the three greatest cultures that have shaped Western man. The dignity and perfection of man lie, for the Greeks, in the intellect; for the Jews, in obedience to the law; for Christians, in love. From the Christian concept of man, enriched by the Greek and Judaic traditions, then, Maritain derives a definition of the aim of education: "to guide man in the evolving dynamism through which he shapes himself as a human person—armed with knowledge, strength of judgment, and moral virtues—while at the same time conveying to him the spiritual heritage of the nation and the civilization" (EC, 10). And since, according to the same philosophical tradition, man's greatest aspirations concern an inner freedom, Maritain further defines the ultimate goal of education as "the conquest of internal and spiritual freedom . . . liberation through knowledge and wisdom, good will, and love" (EC, 11). The liberating of that inner principle of the person's freedom is the sense in which Maritain understands the term "liberal education."

Maritain's philosophy of education thus situates itself firmly in the humanist tradition. It leaves no room for the pragmatist's concept of conditioned response, a doctrine that sees education as a kind of animal training. For Maritain, this perversion of education arises from a widespread confusion between two distinct aspects of man's freedom for development: his individuality and his personality. The former refers to the material ego, the preconditioned instincts through which man develops on the plane of a nonrational animal, a material organism. Now, the specifically human aspect of man lies in his spiritual condition as a unique soul and in his freedom as a rational creature with free will. This rational-spiritual aspect is identified by Maritain as personality. When the educator sees man as individual rather than personality, he "reduces the education and progress of man to the mere freeing of the material ego" (EC, 35). The essential conquest of inner freedom in the student is, rather, a "human awakening," the freeing of his personality, which expresses his most profoundly human aspirations.

In line with this concept of liberal education, Maritain perceives the immense importance of the fundamental pedagogical principle of student-oriented teaching. Learning, after all, can only take place in the student, regardless of the erudition of his instructor. Data that have been neatly sorted and translated into adult formulae cannot be injected into the passive, receptive learner. In a thoroughly humanized learning experience, the teacher feels a genuine concern and respect for the student, "a sort of sacred and loving attention to his mysterious identity, which is a hidden thing that no techniques can reach" (EC, 9). This concept of learning naturally arises from an understanding of the mystery involved in the act of knowing.

"Teaching is an art; the teacher is an artist" (EC, 30). Here is one of the great aphorisms of Maritain's writing. If a teacher has a proper appreciation for the mysterious identity of his student, he can indeed approach education as an art. But not the art of Michelangelo, which required the artist to impose a preconceived form on the clay or stone. Instead, Maritain compares teaching to the art of medicine, a cooperative art in which the essential dynamic principle is that of nature. The doctor simply works to create the conditions that will facilitate the healing process, for which nature, not he, is responsible. The doctor is thus subservient to nature. And, similarly, the teacher—subservient to the intellectual vitality within the student—works to foster the free flowering of that inner principle.

Furthermore, Maritain makes a quite firm endorsement of the principle of the universal right to education. Democracy, he affirms, depends upon the education of the masses and cannot be served properly by an elitist educational philosophy. Government of the people, by the people, and for the people is not practicable without a populace whose understanding of natural law, human rights, and the function of government is at a minimum level of sophistication. For the same reason, too, the technocratic influence on modern education would be particularly pernicious to a democracy, since overspecialization in education would lead to the common man's abdication from political involvement. If government were left only to political specialists, the political arena would be dehumanized, and democracy would fall prey to a form of materialism that denies the capacity of human reason to cope with the diversity of modern life.

II   *A New Curriculum*

With education thus defined and understood, Maritain also gives more specific rules by which the educator may preserve the humanizing effect of his teaching. First, he must accentuate the positive. By laying emphasis on encouragement rather than enforcement whenever possible, he can best liberate the good energies inherent in the student. Second, he must stress the inward growth of the learner. The student must strive to know the essential meaning of his subject matter in itself rather than learn music, for example, only in order to become a composer. Next, the educator should promote the unity between manual work or training and mental growth. And, finally, it is necessary to work always for the student's rational mastery over things learned. That is, searching must never be valued at the expense of finding, and the teacher should never leave a question unanswered on the specious pretext that the mental exercise involved in the quest is more important than arriving at the solution.

In refusing to grant questioning the same educational value as resolving, Maritain is led to another point that is not unrelated. Mental gymnastics do not fulfill the learner's intellectual thirst as truth freely apprehended can, and there is in the curriculum of a liberal education an order, a hierarchy, that must not be ignored. Various scholastic subjects have varying degrees of worth to the learner, and not just practical utility. Maritain calls knowledge of most worth the subjects that make "the mind penetrate into those things that are the richest in truth and intelligibility" (EC,

51). In this sense, he says, subjects with more knowledge value are of the most worth and those with more training value are of less worth. Still these latter have their rightful place in the elementary and secondary curriculum, as long as they are seen in the proper perspective. Among those subjects of value principally as training he includes play, an activity whose worth is enhanced in Maritain's view by the element of free creativity—even of poetry—that it involves. It takes a poet's sensibility to point out this kind of detail in a philosophy of education. Today's progressive educators would no doubt be impressed by the activities Maritain includes under this rubric, expanding play to not only games and sports but handcrafts, mechanics, gardening, beekeeping, rustic lore, cooking, and home economics.

Maritain gives a general outline of his own version of the hierarchy of the curriculum, based on his epistemological theory—"the degrees of knowledge"—and the psychological stages of growth in man. In childhood, the elementary schools should teach the "pre-liberal arts": principally, grammar, logic, history, and geography. The liberal arts proper are introduced at the secondary and college level, when the students are at the adolescent stage of growth. Maritain's recasting of the liberal arts is presented in the light of modern scientific and philosophical developments, but not to the detriment of classical learning. "Our *trivium*," he says, "would concern the creative activity of the mind—truth to be perceived and assented to 'according to the worth of evidence' " (EC, 57). It includes mathematics, physics and the natural sciences, speculative philosophy, and practical philosophy.

Maritain's ideas on curriculum are of special significance to the contemporary scene in American higher education. The wave of curricular liberalism that came on the heels of student activism in the late 1960s has left its mark on many campuses where students are now free to study practically any courses that suit their fancy. Conversely, they may avoid those that do not appeal to them. For Maritain, educators have a responsibility to determine curriculum. He quotes Robert Hutchins's *The Higher Learning of America,* insisting that if educators leave the choice of curriculum to students, they are, in effect, confessing "that they are nothing but chaperons, supervising an aimless, trial-and-error process which is chiefly valuable because it keeps young people from doing something worse." (Quoted in EC, 65 n.)

Maritain advocates a rearrangement of the sequence of scholastic levels to fit the three stages of growth earlier mentioned. Elementary education would end at age twelve. Secondary school would last three years (ages thirteen through fifteen), in which the "pre-liberal arts" would all be studied, with the exception of logic. The college experience would cover ages sixteen through nineteen, the four years to be organized thusly: year 1—mathematics and poetry; year 2—natural science and fine arts; year 3—philosophy; and year 4—ethical and political philosophy. This is, of course, only an outline of the main curricular emphases. Each year of studies, in fact, includes mathematics, literature, and poetry, among other things. One conspicuous absence in this curriculum is Greek and Latin, which Maritain prefers to save for graduate students in languages, literature, history, or philosophy. It is rather surprising to hear a traditionalist like Maritain assert that below the graduate level "they would represent chiefly a waste of time for the many destined to forget them" (EC, 69). However, he stresses the value of classical literature to be read in translation. Modern foreign languages, on the other hand, are to be studied from age ten through secondary school, so that upon entering college, the empirical knowledge of the language is already mastered and the student may proceed to a more rational and logical analysis of the intellectual nourishment made available to him by his language proficiency.

III *Education and the Crisis of Modern Culture*

Among the special trials of education in the contemporary era, Maritain saw the split between religion and life as crucial. To this he attributed such diverse problems as the plight of modern philosophy, the decline of family life, and the crisis in political conscience. Francis Fergusson has said that Maritain's work is especially helpful to someone who is bewildered by the modern philosophical climate of knowledge and skepticism. It is a kind of reorienting of the dazed modern mind toward timeless truths. In analogous fashion, Maritain's idea of an integral education is designed to free the human person from the fragmenting tendencies of a philosophy enslaved by science, or of thought controlled by action. It takes cognizance of the fact that "the most crucial problem with which our educational system is confronted is not a problem of education, but of civilization."[2]

The modern educator must not allow technology to devour the humanities. He must integrate physics and mathematics into the liberal arts and teach the whole curriculum as a unified body of knowledge and wisdom. The humanities—for here again Maritain scrupulously defines his terms—are understood as "those disciplines which make man more human . . . because they convey to him the spiritual fruit and achievements of the labor of generations, and deal with things which are worth being known for their own sake, for the sake of truth or the sake of beauty" (EM, 84). And since Maritain takes seriously the biblical assertion that it is the truth that sets man free, his idea of a liberal education necessarily entails also the teaching of democratic principles, good citizenship, morals, and even theology.

Permissiveness, for Maritain, is no way to purge youngsters of their more primitive instincts. There is a need for authority in education, both intellectual authority to instruct and moral authority to be respected. When modern culture approaches the point where, "exhausted and bewildered by dint of false and dehumanized philosophy, reason confesses its impotence to justify any ethical standards" (EC, 94), then what is needed are teachers with high moral standards (for civic morality) and especially the family influence (for personal morality). The school must first and foremost be concerned with teaching young people to think, not with forming their moral character. This latter task is primarily incumbent upon the family and the spiritual community. But the school has a responsibility for moral teaching, too, because knowledge is a prerequisite for virtue. Education's impact on the will is indirect but crucial because it supplies "the intellectual foundations of moral life" (EM, 105). Real authority, moreover, does not tend to make education into a process of creating an ideal type of person. It doesn't border on despotic educational philosophies. Rather, it entails an honest recognition by youth of the right, on the part of authority, to be obeyed, and the recognition by authority of the goal of liberating the principle of free development in the human person.

Maritain uses two arguments to support his claim that religion and theology have their rightful place in the curriculum, even in public schools. He acknowledges the fact that a religious minority, or even majority, in a school is not entitled to impose its beliefs on others. But by this very same reasoning he insists that "we have no right to impose our own areligious or irreligious philosophy on our fellow-citizens" (EM, 77). Indeed, how unfair it would be to deprive today's youth of any area of knowledge they need in order to cope with the chaotic modern world! He therefore advocates devoting some part of the instructional schedule to religious teaching by a faculty who belong to the main denominations and who would be teaching students of their own denomination. Students of an atheistic persuasion would be allowed to study comparative religion. Aside from this moral aspect of the issue, Maritain also cites the argument that the full growth of the intellect is incomplete without theology, for knowledge includes theology. In fact, to anyone who admits of the validity of a religion, theology is the supreme science, the highest use one can make of reason. Among the degrees of knowledge, it is inferior only to mystical wisdom.

The democratic way of life—its source and doctrines—is still another aspect of the curriculum to which Maritain gives special importance. It is an essential part of the philosophical heritage that undergirds the humanities and without which a liberal education would be doomed to failure in the modern world. It requires a group of teachers who believe unequivocally in the "democratic charter," and who will teach it as a fruition of culture and history, as integrated into the lives and teaching of the great poets, thinkers, and heroes of the past. It must be studied in a manner consonant with the pluralistic principle, but should not be arbitrarily cut off from the religious and philosophical values from which it has drawn its inspiration.

The humanistic tradition of education, of liberal education, is thus renewed and reinvigorated by Maritain's Thomism. He analyzes the process of education in the humanist context as essentially twofold, a process of two dynamisms that must be properly balanced. First, and most important, there is the flowering of the inborn spiritual and rational freedom of the personality, the growth of the person, without which there is no impetus and no spontaneity. Second, this free development must be discreetly and lovingly guided by an appreciation of past efforts—triumphs and failures—along the same lines. Free development of human creativity and an acquaintance with one's cultural heritage—these are the indispensable goals of Maritain's "integral education for an integral humanism."

CHAPTER 7

Philosophy of History

M ARITAIN'S practical philosophy also addressed from time
to time the problem of history, although never at great length
or in any exhaustively systematic fashion. It is inevitable that a
moral philosopher of his importance should touch often on the
meaning of history, but he never found the opportunity to
articulate a formal philosophy of history. The most fully detailed
account on this subject is found in *On the Philosophy of
History,*[1] which Joseph Evans edited from taped recordings of a
series of lectures Maritain had given at the University of Notre
Dame in 1955.

In the final pages of this book, Maritain observes that it
features a rather heavy emphasis on the "supraphilosophical
data" upon which philosophy depends for a perspective on the
past. And he goes on to indicate that a more systematic formu-
lation of his own philosophy of history would entail of necessity
a more careful analysis of the "merely natural aspects of the
philosophy of history, especially as concerns the comparative
study of civilizations" (PH, 171). One would expect the primacy
of the spiritual in Maritain's philosophy to dictate an emphasis
on the importance of supraphilosophical data for the philosophy
of history, and such is indeed the case. It can only be lamented
that he never found the right time to give a more protracted
consideration to the philosophy of history, for the conclusions
that he draws rather briefly in these final pages on the work of
Spengler and Toynbee are vigorously provocative.

I *Contrasting Philosophies of History*

Spengler is unceremoniously dismissed as "a rather questionable wisdom-monger." Toynbee is discussed more seriously, but
fares little better at the hands of the Thomist system. Maritain
pays due respect to the thoroughness and erudition of Toynbee's

work, but finds it ultimately disappointing principally because it seeks to understand human history from a totally anthropocentric humanist perspective. Those all-important supraphilosophical data are woefully absent from Toynbee's picture of history. And yet, as Maritain sees it, Toynbee betrays a fundamental inconsistency when he gives to religion a place of immense importance in the evolution of civilization: "Though Toynbee sees civilization, at least in its higher forms, as receiving its meaning from religion and as oriented toward religion, still he finally conceives religion as itself subservient to civilization, because for him the mission of religion is not defined wth respect to God and divine truth, but rather with respect to mankind" (PH, 176).

The basic disagreement between Maritain and these philosophers of history lies in his definition of the philosophy of history as a field of knowledge. Placing it in the context of the degrees of knowledge, which are so well outlined in his epistemological theory, Maritain holds that history is not a purely empirical science in the sense that nineteenth century positivism would have one believe. The spurious philosophies of history are already misled when they seek to explain history, to master it intellectually. This Maritain sees as another manifestation of modern philosophy's tendency to appropriate the attitude of the empirical sciences toward reality. History, he insists, must not be considered a problem to be solved, but a mystery to be progressively enlightened. Philosophers can no more explain history than theologians can explain the Trinity. In the Thomist view, then, philosophy of history is connatural, experiential knowledge. It is a deeper knowledge of experience than merely factual history, a final application of philosophical truths to the entire movement of humanity. And all this is perceived in the light of important theological truths, so that it is essentially a moral philosophy.

The most formidable opponent for a Christian philosophy of history must be Hegel, if one judges from Maritain's *On the Philosophy of History*. Hegel invented philosophy of history as a conscious philosophical discipline, but he fell prey to historical gnosticism, the delusion of giving a definitive explanation of the movement of history. His greatest intuitive discovery was that history is essentially dynamic; it is concerned, of necessity, with movement and change. But Hegel's dialectics interpreted the movement of history as cyclical and became all too narrowly bound to the notion of determinism.

The Christian philosophy of history, on the other hand, begins in an unselfconscious way with St. Augustine's *City of God,* which offers the first interpretation of time and human history as linear. Christianity teaches that history is characterized by a linear movement toward a determined consummation that is final. As such, Christian philosophy was the first wisdom to come to terms with the irrevocable nature of death, not only for the individual but also for the world. Primitive cultures had refused to face the meaning of death by rationalizing it into myths of cyclical recurrence, reincarnation, etc. So Christian thought made an immensely important contribution to the advancement of philosophy by its acceptance of time and history.

Auguste Comte and even Marx shared Hegel's overemphasis on determinism. They failed to acknowledge sufficiently the role of human freedom in history. Maritain admits that certain great trends in history are determined and necessary. He cites the technological development of society as an example. But he insists that the manner in which such trends are allowed to take shape, the way they are ushered in, is determined by man's freedom. In other words, laws of history are necessary; events are contingent.

One good historical example of the interplay of necessity and human freedom is the Marxist revolution in Russia. Maritain states that the sociopolitical conditions in Europe in the late nineteenth century cried out for a revolution. A revolution in behalf of the industrial proletariat was a historical inevitability. What was not a historical necessity was the Marxist character of the revolution. If, he surmises, there had been in Europe at that time a kind of Christian Gandhi with a well-evolved political philosophy, that inevitable upheaval could have taken the form of a Christian social revolution.

The great fallacy of Hegel's theory of history and of all immanentist theories (those which "explain" history in terms of atheistic humanism), is that they insist that the only reality is becoming, endless change, and yet "they offer themselves as the definitive and final revelation, at the end of time, of the meaning of all history" (PH, 162). The Christian philosopher never encounters such an inconsistency, since, for him, the end is beyond time.

II *Fundamental Laws of Historical Evolution*

All the above matters could be characterized, like the title of Maritain's book, as his thought "on" the philosophy of history. In other words, they are concerned with defining what philosophy of history is and isn't and with analyzing other philosophies of history. Moving on to the actual application of Thomist philosophy to history—that is, thoughts "in" the philosophy of history—one finds that, for Maritain, history proceeds according to certain laws that may be observed by the moral philosopher.

The most fundamental of these laws is what he calls "the law of two-fold contrasting progress." It is altogether different from the eighteenth century notion that man is bound by fate to ever-ascending knowledge and mastery of all the challenges of life. This naive overconfidence led to a tendency to consider the new always superior to the old, a tendency that has proved pernicious in Western culture. For although the West has seen astounding advances in empirical sciences and technology in modern times (and this Maritain sees as one of those necessary trends of history), there has been far too little progress in man's ability to deal with the more fundamental problems of life—the philosophical and spiritual problems whose solutions determine the manner in which those technological innovations are to be used.

To illustrate the law of twofold contrasting progress, Maritain uses the parable of Matthew 13: 24 - 30, in which Christ compares the kingdom of heaven to a field where the owner sowed good seed and his enemy sowed cockle. The workers in the field are alarmed at the growing cockle. But the owner instructs them not to weed, for fear of cutting the young grain. For he knows that at harvest time he can have them separate the two, keeping the good grain and burning the cockle. Certain events of history appear to be exclusively beneficial or detrimental to the cause of man, but they always have an opposite, more hidden effect. "The Christian knows that, though constantly thwarted and constantly concealed, the work of the spirit is carried out in spite of everything, as history goes on, and that thus from fall to fall, but also from obscure gain, time marches toward the resurrection" (PH, 45). For example, the past two hundred years of political history have witnessed great progress in the winning of human rights, social justice, and liberty, but they have also seen the rise of totalitarianism (both communist and fascist), racism, and wars of unprecedented cost to human life.

Maritain sees the first great insight into the direction and meaning of history in the writings of St. Paul. According to Paul's divinely inspired teachings, the three historical states of existential man morally considered are (1) the state of nature, (2) the state of Ancient Law, and (3) the state of the New Law—the latter two referring to Jewish and Christian law respectively. Within this context, Maritain reiterates Paul's prophetic doctrine of the destiny of the Jewish people, found in Romans 9 - 11. Israel rejected the Messiah and thus fell from God's calling, but their fall was for the divine purpose of the salvation of all mankind. God used their alienation for the reconciliation of the Gentiles. But their alienation was only temporary, and one of the signs of the final stage of history will be their full reintegration. In the context of the temporal history of the world, Maritain sees Israel's role as an "earthly leavening." Israel's chosen task is "to irritate the world, to prod it, to move it. It teaches the world to be dissatisfied and restless so long as it has not God, so long as it has not justice on earth" (PH, 92).

This doctrine figures prominently in theological speculation throughout the Middle Ages and is more fully delineated by Thomas Aquinas, and it is especially important in considerations of Christian eschatology. Maritain himself was fascinated with the "mystery of Israel," as he called it, and he returned to it repeatedly—in *Ransoming the Time, The Living Thoughts of Saint Paul,* and, for example, *A Christian Looks at the Jewish Question.*

Another law of history that Maritain elaborates is that of the passing of human knowledge from a magical state in primitive culture into a rational state in modern culture. Here he takes issue with Auguste Comte and other positivists who make the magic and rational or scientific forms of knowledge "essentially inimical and incompatible." For Maritain, primitive man possessed in a magical state "all the mental and cultural functions of the human being," just as these same functions now exist in a primarily rational state. Using the work of modern anthropologists, he shows that modern man has not "outgrown" the forms of knowledge often associated with magic—mystical experience, metaphysics, and poetry. Conversely, the intellect of primitive

man, although "involved with, and dependent on, the imagination and its savage world," accomplished in the magical state
essentially the same functions that modern science does today.

Among the other laws of history outlined by Maritain, one is
especially struck by the progressive nature of man's knowledge
of moral laws. Maritain clearly distinguishes between progress in
human moral behavior and knowledge of the norms of natural
law. Abraham, he points out, "was a very great saint, with an
absolutely pure heart" (PH, 106). Abraham's response to what
he knew of natural law was superior, but the norms of moral law
today are much more demanding. Modern man is not superior
in purity to Abraham, but the intervening centuries of human
history have left him with a more advanced knowledge of what
natural law prescribes in a given situation.

III *God and History*

A final section of *On the Philosophy of History* concerns the
relation of God and history, obviously a question of fundamental importance for interpreting the events and trends of
human history. The highly controversial issue of human free will
and divine providence is involved in this discussion, which
Maritain begins by emphasizing that God is "in absolutely no
way the cause of moral evil" (PH, 119). In this passage, as he
also explains more fully in *Existence and the Existent,*[2] one is to
understand that moral evil originates in man's free decision to
ignore God's plan, in his "free nihilation" of the divine rule. At
the same time God's plan accounts in advance for man's
"initiatives of nihilating." This is one of the senses in which
Maritain interprets the biblical sayings of Christ: "Without me
you can do nothing." Not only does the statement mean that
man is powerless without God; it also means that "without God
we can do nothingness, i.e., without God we can make the thing
which is nothing, we can introduce into action and being the
nothingness which wounds them and which constitutes evil"
(PH, 122).

According to this basic doctrine in which God provides the
first initiative for good, and man, for evil, good is also initiated
in a secondary manner by created human freedom. It forms the
basis on which a definition of history is founded. "History is
made up above all of the crossing and intermingling, of the

pursuit and conflict of uncreated liberty and created liberty. It is, as it were, invented at each moment by the accorded or dis-accorded initiatives of these two freedoms" (PH, 123). The philosopher of history, in the unaided light of human reason, can perceive the intricate design of such a relationship only as if through a glass darkly. And that is why he cannot presume to explain history.

Drawing again on the Thomist tradition, Maritain suggests three aspects of the end of human history in the secular context. As prophesied in Genesis 1:28, man will continue to progress toward mastery over nature and conquest of political autonomy. He will be less and less enslaved by physical nature or by other men. Second, he will continue the advance in "the self-perfecting activities" of his being, i.e., knowledge in all realms, artistic creativity, and knowledge of natural law. Finally, he will move closer to "the manifestation of all the potentialities of human nature." The source for this historical interpretation is Matthew 10:26: "There is nothing hidden which shall not be made manifest." And an interesting application that Maritain makes of it is his notion that the often shocking explicitness of contemporary art, despite its dubious motives and modish tendencies, is partly the fulfillment of the third aspect of the end of human history, that desire to make manifest whatever is within man.

IV *The Future Directions of History*

Perhaps the most provocative speculations that Maritain has made on the future course of history are found in *Integral Humanism.* These ideas grow out of his observations on the growth of modern sociopolitical and economic systems. Social-ism, he believes, arose by way of a natural reaction to capitalist abuses, and it has had certain beneficial effects on civilization, namely, a growth in awareness, or class consciousness. Alongside this historical gain in awareness of the dignity of the worker, however, the tragedy of that same historical movement is that such a spiritual gain should have been accomplished by an atheistic system.

Christians in the twentieth century have come to recognize in the proletariat a "bearer of fresh moral reserves which assign to it a mission in regard to the new world" (IH, 235). The most crucial issue to be resolved in the near future is whether the proletariat will be increasingly bound to a philosophy of materialism with the metaphysical errors it entails or whether it will find a new philosophy in the principles of Christianity, a necessarily theocentric humanism. That issue, which Maritain enlightened so significantly for the emerging Latin American nations late in his career, is now becoming equally important in the African continent, among other points on the shrinking globe.

The realization of a Christian humanist political order appears improbable to Maritain before a universal political upheaval, which he regards as inevitable anyway. Man is still, he says, "in a pre-historic age" insofar as accomplishing the refraction of the Gospel in the temporal realm. But the next age of history he sees as the third era of civilization since Christ: the first being Christian antiquity, which reached its zenith in medieval times; the second, the "modern" age, characterized by a dissolution of the first; and the third, upon whose threshold man is not yet standing, to witness the flowering of a humanism of the Incarnation—still not a definitive form of integral humanism, but rather an essentially progressive one.

CHAPTER 8

Art Theory and Criticism

M ARITAIN'S widest notoriety stems from his vastly influential political and social philosophy; yet his concern with the realm of art manifested itself even before he began to become involved in other branches of practical philosophy. One of the most important books of his early career is *Art and Scholasticism,* which appeared first in 1920. In subsequent editions of this book there were added *The Frontiers of Poetry* and other essays and notes on contemporary artists. In 1926, Cocteau's *Lettre à Jacques Maritain* and Maritain's *Réponse à Jean Cocteau* enlarged the applications of the Thomist doctrine of art and reached more deeply into the literary public.[1] Other important works by Maritain on art include *The Situation of Poetry* (1938), in which Raïssa contributed two chapters, and *The Responsibility of the Artist* (1960). The most masterful compendium of his observations on art, however, is *Creative Intuition in Art and Poetry* (1953). Maritain's preoccupation with the problems of writers, painters, and musicians spanned the major part of his career, and it grew into one of the most important aspects of his writing.

The first three sections of this chapter will focus upon three texts: *Art and Scholasticism, The Responsibility of the Artist,* and *Creative Intuition in Art and Poetry,* in that order. With each text, discussion of Maritain's critical judgments will be deferred until the last section of the chapter.

I The Thomist Doctrine of Art

In *Art and Scholasticism,*[2] Maritain brought an entirely different perspective to the world of contemporary art. During World War I, the Dada experiment had jolted the public with its message of antiart. In 1924, André Breton had expressed the aesthetics of the new wave of artists in his *Manifesto of Surreal-*

103

ism. Into this world of disorientingly novel interpretations Maritain introduced the question: Why not return to the ideas of the Greeks, to Aristotle, to Plato, for the philosophical basis upon which to build a sound doctrine of art? For this is exactly where his master Saint Thomas had turned in the thirteenth century when he had given his own views on aesthetic problems. The result of this reorienting is one of the most original and enlightening bodies of aesthetic thought to be found in the modern era.

Since there existed no single treatise in which the scholastics discoursed on art as such, Maritain's task was first to compile the basic aesthetic ideas of such masters as Aristotle and Plato, Albertus Magnus, Cajetan, Denis the Areopagite, and especially Thomas Aquinas. Next, he turned to the contemporary literary and artistic scene and applied the philosophically constructed scholastic theory of art to specific works and movements with brilliant insight. His theoretical method was thus firmly grounded and the scope of his criticism proved virtually universal.

The formal articulation of the Thomist doctrine of art comprises the main body of *Art and Scholasticism* and is recapitulated in chapter two of *Creative Intuition*. Here one finds that the schoolmen's definition of art was much broader than the modern concept. Rather than confining it to the realm of fine arts, the scholastics considered art to include such activities as shipbuilding and clockmaking. In other words, for the scholastics, the artist was first and foremost an artisan, a craftsman.

Art being a function of the intelligence, it is important to distinguish between the speculative and practical orders of the intelligence. In the speculative order, the intelligence seeks pure knowledge for its own sake; it is the most proper function of the intelligence. The practical order seeks knowledge as a means toward the accomplishment of some action it has in view. The perfect joy of the speculative intellect lies in the contemplation of the divine essence. But man's reason usually operates in the practical order toward the achievement of certain human ends.

The most important distinction Maritain draws in *Art and Scholasticism* is the one that contrasts the two spheres within the practical intellect: the sphere of doing *(agibile)* and the sphere of making *(factible)*. According to the schoolmen, doing consists in the pure exercise of our free will. An action in this sphere is good if it conforms to the true end of human existence. It is the sphere of morality, controlled by prudence, the virtue of the practical intellect that "measures our acts with regard to an ultimate end which is God himself sovereignly loved" (AS, 7).

Making, on the other hand, is the productive action in relation to the thing to be produced, and an action in this sphere is good only if it conforms to the work to be made, which is its sole and independent end. Art is the virtue that controls this sphere. Art remains outside the human sphere and orders all action according to the intellectual form of the work to be made. The role of art in making is analogous to that of prudence in doing: "Prudence works for the good of the one acting. . . . Art works for the good of the work made" (AS, 15). Art cannot be concerned with the moral value of the artist's action, for the end of art lies in the work to be produced. And since making is independent of doing, art "delivers one from the human" and places the artist "in a world apart, closed, limited, absolute" (AS, 9). This distinction between doing and making, which Maritain borrowed from the scholastics, is of central importance to his aesthetics. Because of this distinction, he was able to put art and morality in proper perspective and to analyze with a new clarity the conflicts they produce in the life of the artist.

Understood in this way, even the most humble artisan has an inherent spiritual dignity; his work is a reflection and a continuation of God's creation. The rules of his work remain outside the human sphere, and abstractly considered in his role of artist, he is essentially amoral. In the Middle Ages the artist was ideally no more than an artisan, and his work was a means of worshiping God. He was unconscious of his spiritual dignity. The Renaissance, in revealing to him his grandeur, also brought to light the conflicts between art and prudence, between his virtues as creator and as moral agent. The first great example of the artist victimized by these agonizing conflicts was Michelangelo; one of the most significant modern examples was Baudelaire.

The fine arts, unlike art in general, are not engaged in the creation of a work that serves essentially utilitarian purposes. In the fine arts, the artist aims to create a work of beauty. And beauty is defined as a shining forth of intelligible form that touches off a sense of delight in the intelligence. For in the work of beauty, the intelligence finds its own light reflected in the well-proportioned wholeness of matter fashioned by the artist.

Beauty, because it is a reflection of divine beauty, belongs to the transcendental, metaphysical order. And it is this spirituality of beauty that enables art to elevate the soul beyond physical reality. Still, art remains in the sphere of making and only leads the soul toward spiritual joy by means of a work enslaved to matter.

On the rules of art, Maritain shows that Aristotle was too narrowly interpreted by the theorists of the seventeenth century, France's Golden Age. The supreme rule of art is that the artist love what he is making. "Thus art, like love, proceeds from a spontaneous instinct, and it must be cultivated like friendship" (AS, 41). In order to cultivate his art, all the artist's desires must be channeled toward beauty by the virtue of art that inhabits him. It is in this sense that he must love what he is making. In the words of Alfred Sisley, "Every picture shows a spot with which the artist himself has fallen in love."[3] Maritain compares the poet's affective relationship to the experience of beauty with Saint Augustine's law of the perfect soul: "Love and do what you want." The analogous law for the artist is: "Cling to your creative intuition, and do what you want" (CI, 60).

The pages of *Art and Scholasticism* concerning the purity of art are a highpoint in Maritain's work. Here, undoubtedly, he was especially inspired by the example of Georges Rouault, the friend who had suffered so much in order to defend the purity of his painting from the temptation to please the public. Art is an essentially spiritual virtue and its purity must be defended from any degrading influence, such as the excessive importance of technical dexterity or the servile imitation of reality. Art suggests, rather than giving a conceptual expression of, something; it does not copy God's creation, but continues it.

Similarly, any philosophical thesis imposed on a work of art tends to corrupt its transcendence. The presence of a particular idea in a work must be entirely natural, not consciously forced. For example, it would be impossible to create an expressly Christian work of art. For Maritain, Christian art can only result when a profoundly and sincerely Christian person creates a beautiful work in which he expresses himself. It is the work of an artist possessed by divine love.

In the final chapter of *Art and Scholasticism,* Maritain examines the interpenetrations of the spheres of making and doing in order to explore the perplexing conflicts between art and morality. In its own sphere art is sovereign, but insofar as it inhabits man and man makes use of it, it is subordinated to the end of man. Prudence is thus superior to art in the human sphere, for an artist is first and foremost a man. But art—which is transcendental because its goal is a work of beauty—art is metaphysically superior to prudence. Prudence is not competent to judge poetic values, and art cannot judge human values. Wisdom alone, which rules both doing and making, is capable of bringing art and prudence harmoniously together. And it is from the lofty transcendence of wisdom that Maritain many years later developed the ethics of art in detail in his *The Responsibility of the Artist* (1960).

II   *The Ethics of Art*

In this last book on art and morality, Maritain begins by stating clearly that an integral approach to the problem must be conducted primarily from the perspective of moral philosophy. Thus, he refutes from the outset the profession so often heard from the lips of modern artists that morality is a branch of aesthetics. Here Maritain explores all the reciprocal relationships among the artist, his work, his society, and his God.

The devotion of the artist to the work to be produced must remain pure, even if the content of his work has an apparent potential for corrupting or degrading the public. He cannot forcibly purify his work by attempting to change its moral nature: "For an artist to spoil his work and sin against his art is forbidden by his artistic conscience."[4] There are only two alternatives. He may simply give up his art, or he may commit himself to "purify the source," so that his artistic vision will naturally tend in a different direction.

Similarly, Maritain shows that the purity of art is again compromised when the artist makes himself subservient to an ideology, as in the case of engaged art *(art engagé)*. Existentialist art can only be propaganda; it abuses and debilitates the creative intellect. "An artist who yields to this craving for regimentation fails by the same token in his gifts, in his calling, and in his proper virtue" (RA, 73).

But the purity of art has sometimes been understood in a perverted sense, as in the example of "Art for Art's sake." The source of the confusion in this nineteenth century literary move-

ment was an excessively abstract notion of the artist purely
as artist, and distinct from his role as man. The phrase "Art
for Art's sake," according to Maritain, is an absurdity. Art
cannot exist in a pure form, cut off from the source of its
creative energy and nourishment, which lie in the matter of
human life. It exists not for its own sake, but for the sake of the
work to be produced, a work that already contains human ideas
and concerns in its organic unity, since it is born not in a
vacuum but in the creative intellect of an artist who is first a
man.

While Maritain defends the purity of art, he also speaks of the
necessity to protect society from misguided or unscrupulous
"artists" who sometimes foist aberrant views of human problems on a public that is not prepared (or inclined) to deal with
them. Here he is careful to insist that limitations on free expression in art should always respect the basic dignity of the intellect
and that the role of the human community at large is far more
important than that of the state. Indeed, expression of public
opinion and free discussion of the controversial works by responsible critics are preferable to excessive involvement of the state
in matters of the creative intellect.

In considering all these problems Maritain reminds his reader
not to think of the artist and his social community as being in
some kind of essential enmity. Art is, rather, necessary to society
because it reminds man of his spiritual nature and teaches him to
come closer to his own vision of the eternal. Moreover, society
also has a responsibility toward art; it must respect it for its
spiritual value and cultivate an interest in the new expressions of
its creativity.

Baudelaire was an artist who was condemned by the state for
the corrupting influence of his work. But he is also an important
example of how time, while not redeeming the poet, has
redeemed his work. In the case of morally dangerous artists,
Maritain says that the depth of their creative experience is what
matters above all rather than the immediate moral impact of
their work. What might indeed have been morally dangerous in
Les Fleurs du mal to the French public of 1857 has lost its
corrupting influence for us today. "The clearest result of
Baudelaire has been to turn modern poetry toward the universe
of the spirit, and to awaken in man a theological sense" (RA,
87).

III   *The Mystery of Artistic Creation*

The birth of a poem or a painting in the creative intelligence of the artist is one of the most fascinating mysteries of human existence. It is a process that cannot be satisfactorily explained by science, and yet poets have usually been too vaguely impressionistic in trying to evoke such an experience. Jacques Maritain had the ideal qualifications of one who would explore this mystery in all its dark complexities: an intellect with sharp analytical powers, the soul and sensibility of a poet, and a remarkable gift for expressing himself with grace and clarity. His concept of knowledge as an "intelligible mystery" enabled him to find a proper balance between the importance of free spontaneity and the discipline of the intellect in the act of poetic creation. *Creative Intuition in Art and Poetry* may well prove to be his most important book. It is certainly among those in which he has applied the Thomist philosophy with the greatest degree of freedom and originality, and thus it bears the stamp of his own personality in a unique way.

Various commentators have been surprised by the breadth of artistic materials used with such profound understanding by Maritain. In addition to citing a myriad of artists on art, poets on poetry, etc., in the main body of the book, he used a dual illustration method, supplying both reproductions of painting and sculpture and what he has called "texts without comment." The latter consist of quotations from great writers who have been especially enlightening to Maritain. This device serves to fulfill one of Maritain's self-proclaimed objectives for his book, namely a kind of "joint tribute" to the poetry of the French and English languages.

Beginning, as he so often does, with working definitions of basic terms, Maritain suggests a conception of poetry that enables him to consider the subject in its most universal terms. Poetry is most essentially "that intercommunication between the inner being of things and the inner being of the human Self which is a kind of divination . . . the secret life of each and all of the arts; another name for what Plato called mousikè" (CI, 3). The mutual knowledge, on a spiritual level, of the self of the artist and the world of nature, of reality, or of things is the experience that lies at the heart of any expression of creativity.

In Oriental art, Maritain insists that although the most characteristic tendency historically has been to express, through a radical elimination of self-consciousness, the objective essence of *things,* the most successful examples of this art betray also the deepest concerns of the creative *self.* And conversely, the modern obsession with self-discovery and self-expression in Western art at its best has revealed also the inner being of things in a new dimension. Although modern nonrepresentational painting has liberated itself from the tyranny of the model, it reveals exterior reality in a more obscure way, for "creative subjectivity cannot awaken to itself except in communing with Things" (CI, 29). Wherever there is poetic experience, says Maritain, there is an interpenetration of things and the self, and a new epiphany of each will be found in the work to be produced.

The creativity of art and poetry is an intellectual activity, as Maritain describes it in *Art and Scholasticism*—art is a virtue of the practical intellect. But in *Creative Intuition in Art and Poetry* he goes deeper into the workings of poetic creation and makes it clear that he is dealing here with a nonconceptual aspect of the human intelligence. In one of his most strikingly original passages, Maritain describes this region of the intellect as the "spiritual unconscious," a faculty of the intellect that is analogous to but entirely separate from the Freudian unconscious. "Far beneath the sunlit surface thronged with explicit concepts and judgments, words and expressed resolutions or movements of the will, are the sources of knowledge and creativity, of love and supra-sensuous desires, hidden in the primordial translucid night of the ultimate vitality of the soul" (CK, 94).

This theory of a spiritual unconscious is a conceptualization of the source of poetry, art, and music in man. The spiritual realm of the intellect that it describes is so easily confused with the Freudian subconscious that poetic experience necessarily entails grave dangers for the soul of the poet, dangers that must be risked with heroic strength and self-sacrifice.

Creative intuition, then, takes place within the spiritual unconscious of the artist by means of what Maritain calls "poetic knowledge." In making the work of art, the artist is always expressing himself, but he cannot express himself without an authentic self-knowledge. And the artist cannot know himself directly as subjectivity. His own subjectivity he can only discover as reflected in the nonconceptual knowledge of the world of things, a "knowledge through affective union . . . or inclination, connaturality or congeniality" (CI, 115 - 17). It is not just rational knowledge, but a form of knowledge that is molded and directed by the will, raised to the poetic level by spiritualized emotion. The mystic's knowledge of God, unlike that of the theologian, is a knowledge through affective union.

Poetic knowledge, thus understood, is directed toward reality "as connatural to the soul pierced by a given emotion" (CI, 126). It is both cognitive and creative, in that it both grasps and expresses reality and the self, but the creative function is of utmost importance, because poetic knowledge can only come to fruition in the work produced. And when reality is grasped and expressed through poetic intuition, it is revealed in a unique way. For "things are not only what they are. They ceaselessly pass beyond themselves, and give more than they have" (CI, 127). Maritain, like Baudelaire, sees the universe as a vast and resonant forest of symbols that can only be deciphered by the poet, the *vates,* the seer. Finally, he observes that poetic intuition cannot be improved or learned through discipline; it can only be more carefully heeded. Poetic intuition depends on the freedom of the creative self, rather than an effort of the conscious will, but its existence within the poet can be fostered by the devotion with which he observes its biddings.

With so much emphasis on the importance of the self in poetic intuition, the question arises whether Maritain sees art as essentially egocentric. The answer lies in his distinction between the creative self and the self-centered ego. This self-centered ego is a defensive, materialistic inclination inward, whereas the creative self is actualized only in an expansiveness and creativity that mirror the giving of one's self that is the essence of love. "Poetry's *I* resembles in this respect the *I* of the saint, and likewise, although to quite other ends, it is a subject which gives" (CI, 143; Maritain's italics).

IV *Beauty*

In Chapter Five, "Poetry and Beauty," Maritain gives still another example of his most characteristic gift—reviving the ideas of scholastic philosophy and applying them to the contemporary world. The doctrine of beauty is here reexamined in the light of Plato, Aristotle, and Aquinas. Beauty is first of all a transcendental; that is, it resists being confined in a class. It

permeates everything, just as goodness, being, and other transcendentals permeate everything. "Thus, just as everything is
good in its own way, so everything is beautiful in its own way"
(CI, 163). In the eyes of God, everything is beautiful to the
extent that it has being.

But this transcendental definition of beauty is not totally
appropriate to the realm of art. For transcendental beauty is
apprehended solely by the intellect, whereas art of necessity
participates in the world of the senses. Beauty perceived by the
senses is aesthetic beauty, and aesthetic beauty does not permeate
all things. As perceived by the senses, indeed many things have
no beauty. So it is that the two categories of beauty must be
distinguished. Ugliness is that which displeases our apprehension
of it, but since God is intellect and has no senses, ugliness does
not exist for Him.

This exposition Maritain offers in order to discuss the proper
relationship of the poet to beauty, with special emphasis on the
development of modern poetry. According to Maritain, it is an
indication of the spiritual tendencies in art that it does not
remain content with aesthetic beauty. "Art endeavors to imitate
in its own way the condition peculiar to pure spirits: it draws
beauty from ugly things and monsters. . . . Art struggles to
surmount the distinction between aesthetic beauty and transcendental beauty and to absorb aesthetic beauty in transcendental
beauty" (CI, 165). Precisely because of this tension between
aesthetic and transcendental beauty, what the poet is striving to
achieve is not simply perfection. Maritain quotes the French poet
Jean Cocteau, who said that beauty limps, and he compares the
idea to Saint Thomas's assertion that contemplation limps.
Jacob, too, limped after his struggle with the angel, because
having experienced the presence of God, his worldly side would
always be noticeably weaker than his spiritual side. Likewise, the
poet remains conscious of the "weaker foot" in his struggle for
beauty, but the limping foot still plays an essential role in his ascent.
In Dante's *Inferno,* the poet begins his pilgrimage toward the
Heavenly Vision with the "firm foot" always lower. That is, he
limps on the weaker left foot, which represents the will. The right
foot, or the intellect, leads the left until at the summit of Mount
Purgatory the will has been purified.

Beauty must be for the poet or artist the end beyond the end,
not the object of his poetic endeavor, but an infinite to be loved

and to be mirrored in the work. When art seeks to produce beauty as its operational end, it degenerates into academicism. Using the Platonic expression, Maritain says that "art engenders in beauty" rather than producing beauty as its object. Beauty is the only atmosphere in which the poet can exist, but his poetic knowledge is directed toward the meeting of reality and the self, and the proper end of his poetic activity is the work to be produced.

V *The Poet, the Mystic, and Inspiration*

The analogy of poetic knowledge to mystical knowledge is one that Maritain uses to elucidate more fully the functioning of creative intuition within the artist. He appropriates Rimbaud's famous visionary utterance, "I is another" *(Je est un autre),* as an expression of the primary law of poetic knowledge—namely, that the subjectivity of the poet, when engaged in poetic knowledge, obscurely identifies itself with a given manifestation of reality. And he quotes a passage from Dante's *Convivio,* which states that "Who paints a figure, if he cannot be it, cannot give form to it."[5] The poet must *become* the subject of his work in order to give it life. It is in this sense that knowledge by connaturality quickens the poetic intuition.

Poetic experience must be understood as distinct from mystical experience, but the two are analogous because they live in close proximity within the spiritual unconscious. And naturally these two realms often become interrelated and penetrate each other in numerous and ambivalent ways. Poetic experience can prepare one for contemplation, but it can also give a nebulous or spurious conception of the nature of contemplation. Mystical experience, on the other hand, can lead the contemplative to ecstatic poetic expression—and often to mediocre poetry. The emotion that activates poetic knowledge is analogous to but distinct from charity in the grace-given experience of the mystic.

No philosophy of art would be complete without a consideration of the proper role of inspiration, and Maritain was well aware of the ongoing debate on this aspect of the poet's craft. His assessment of the problem is predictable in that he grants due importance to the respective elements that must be balanced: inspiration and reason. Like most other important theorists of art, he insists that neither can suffice alone in the artist.

The originality of his treatment of the problem is his rejection of the traditionally accepted concept of the Platonic muse. Inspiration, he asserts, does not come to a passive, totally receptive poet from some source outside his own intelligence. It exists within his own creativity. It is the inner creative energy of the poet's soul that results from a prior phase of quietude and restful concentration. (Maritain calls the two phases "systolic" and "diastolic.") Thus, the poet can prepare himself for the quickening action of inspiration by eliminating discordant elements and disciplining his rational powers to channel into his work only those elements that burn with the fires of poetic intuition. For the weaker of the Romantics, the Platonic concept of inspiration became, according to Maritain, "an excuse for facility, or simple release of brute emotions and passions, or uncontrolled flux of shallow words and sentimentalism" (CI, 243). Unfortunately, this counterfeit doctrine of inspiration has led many modern critics to harbor an unreasonable prejudice against the proper role of inspiration in art.

VI *Music: The Quintessential Source*

In Chapter Eight of *Creative Intuition,* "The Internalization of Music," Maritain describes first the manner in which the preconscious life of the intellect gives birth to a poem. Here he is speaking of the poet in general, in any age. Within the poet's soul there is a "spiritual milieu" in which images and emotions exist in a free and fluid state, ready to be enlisted in the work of poetic creation. At the moment when they are first dimly perceived by the poet, they touch off in him an inaudible melody, a music of dynamic mental charges that Maritain calls "intuitive pulsions." The discovery of this "wordless musical stir" in the poet's spiritual unconscious is at the source of all poetry. This phenomenon he conceptualizes for us in order to speak of the essential difference between classical and modern poetry, the internalization of music in the poem.

In the poet's consciousness and from his own point of view, the music of intuitive pulsions is the source of an irresistible urge for expression, for creativity. These dynamic charges, once they are perceived, demand to be expressed in a work. Hence, the phenomenon of the compulsive writer. Communication and self-expression are not central to him. It suffices for him to give birth to the work; the desire to be heard and understood, while it does indeed exist, is only of secondary importance. As Julien Green has put it, the novelist who truly deserves to be called by that name is the one who would feel obliged to continue to write without being appreciated, or without even the prospect of being published.

From the point of view of the reader, however, communication is obviously of vital importance. Poetic intuition for him becomes cognitive, receptive, rather than creative. The reader of poetry becomes aware of its inaudible music not because of a conceptual understanding of the meaning of a poem, but through the power of the poem to awaken within his soul a melody that is similar to the music of intuitive pulsions that gave birth to it in the poet.

Maritain here stresses the distinction between this wordless music, which is the genesis of a poem, and the audible music of the words in the objectivized form of the finished work. For he is leading up to the central argument of the chapter, in which he contrasts classical and modern poetry on the basis of the increasing importance of the inaudible inner music. In classical poetry, says Maritain, the reader is confronted with two meanings simultaneously: first, a definite set of things susceptible of rational, logical understanding, and second, a flash of reality, grasped by the poet in a nonconceptual manner. The intuitive flash of reality is revealed, then, by the method of "purposive comparison." The poet discovers an image in his consciousness that bears an inherent similarity to some aspect of the flash of reality, and thus compares this image to it in order to give it an intelligible expression. This method characterized classical poetry because of the supreme importance of the logos, of the rational, logical expression of thought and feeling.

By contrast, modern poetry confronts the reader with only the second "meaning" described in classical poetry. Rather than the method of purposive comparison, the modern poet operates by means of the "immediately illuminating image":

Two things are not compared, but rather one thing is made known through the image of another. One thing already known is not brought near to another thing already known. One thing which was unknown — only contained in the obscurity of emotive intuition — is discovered, and

expressed, by means of another already known, and by the same stroke
their similarity is discovered.   (CI, 329)

The audible music of words, which is associated with the
rational, logical meaning in classical poetry, tends to obscure the
music of intuitive pulsions in its most spontaneous, freest form.
But in modern poetry, the wordless musical stir confronts the
reader more directly, unhampered by the exigencies of the logos.
It is thus that modern poetry is more obscure than its classical
equivalent.

VII *Poetic Melody, Theme, and Number*

According to Maritain there are three moments of epiphany
for creative intuition in the process of poetic creation—three
forms in which it appears to the poet in a kind of progressive
incarnation. The first epiphany is what Maritain calls the
melody, or *poetic sense* (without, however, any connotation of a
rational, logical "meaning"). The second form in which intuition
is revealed is the *theme,* or *action,* of the work; and the third
and final form is called *number,* or *harmonic structure.* For the
reader, the order of the three epiphanies is reversed.

These terms would obviously be confusing without precise
definitions, and Maritain, as usual, is careful to make them
clear. The poetic sense is the soul of the poem, consubstantial
with the poetic experience that is the birth of the poem in the
poet's consciousness. It is an inner melody intuitively perceived
by the poet's—or the reader's—creative intelligence. In using the
word "theme," he is thinking of what the poem wills, rather
than what it is. But since a poem can have no volition, he
replaces the term "will" by its analogue in inanimate objects:
namely, "action." Here, he uses extensively the ideas of Francis
Fergusson, whose *The Idea of a Theatre* defines action as
follows: "the focus or aim of psychic life from which the events
. . . result."[6] Maritain quotes Fergusson's definition and adds a
phrase of his own for further clarification—"the spiritual élan"
of the work. He agrees with Fergusson in contrasting this idea of
action with the plot of a work. Finally, the number, or harmonic
structure, of the work is the expansion of creative intuition into
its most consonant proportions—that is, the rhythm, length, and
design of the work of words.

It has often been observed by various literary critics that modern literature, while having discovered a new depth of vibrant poetic spontaneity (what Maritain calls "the internalization of music"), is lacking in strong basic themes. This phenomenon is confirmed by Maritain, and he offers his own explanation for it. Theme in the literary work, he argues, depends to a great extent on the intellectual baggage of the artist. A writer, in expressing the inner promptings of his creativity, expresses of necessity his world view, and a world view in modern times most often lacks coherence. Nowadays the artist's intellectual baggage is usually so diverse as to defy orderly integration.

By contrast, the world view of Dante was so beautifully unified and complete that the action or theme of his *Commedia* is in constant proportional agreement with its inner melody. This great virtue of Dante the poet is what Maritain calls his "creative innocence," a term that should in no wise be confused with moral innocence. It is an ontological innocence that concerns the intuition of the poet rather than his loves. To whatever degree all the philosophical, political, and psychological concepts of the poet as man are consumed in his poetic intuition and made a function of the fire of his creative emotion, to just such a degree may he be said to possess the quality of poetic innocence. This is why Dante is able to avoid boring his readers even though he preaches and didacticizes continually in the *Commedia*. The allegory and the philosophical-theological system in his work are a function of its free creativity; the *Commedia* is primarily a poem that delights, rather than an allegory that teaches. One can intelligently read it with great pleasure without sharing Dante's faith because: "Theological faith itself . . . has entered the work through the instrumentality of creative emotion and poetic knowledge, and passed through the lake of disinterestedness of creative innocence" (CI, 379 - 80).

VIII *Maritain as Critic*

Jacques Maritain never sought for himself the title of critic. In his writings on the arts he always took care to point out that he was expressing himself from the perspective of the philosopher. Consequently, the observations he has made on writers, painters, and musicians are scattered among the pages of the more theoretical works that have formed the material of the above portion of this chapter. In the copious notes and appendixes at the end of *Art and Scholasticism,* and in *The Frontiers of Poetry* —which was included in the 1935 edition of the former title— Maritain applies the Thomist aesthetic doctrine with striking lucidity to modern movements in art. Other texts containing some of his more significant critical judgments include his *Réponse à Jean Cocteau (Art and Faith,* 1926), *The Situation of Poetry* (1938), *Art and Poetry* (1943), *Creative Intuition in Art and Poetry* (1953), and *The Responsibility of the Artist* (1960).

What one finds in Maritain's criticism is consistent with the positions he professed in the various domains of his more strictly philosophical thought. As in his social and political philosophy, he excels in maintaining a stable equilibrium in the heart of a central paradox. And again, the paradox consists of an apparent tension between the structure of thought inherited from the scholastic tradition and the creative application and extension by Maritain of this structure to contemporary contexts. He remains traditionalist in the sense of his faithfulness to Thomist thought, but he also demonstrates a surprising modernity in his profoundly sympathetic analysis of the work of recent writers and painters. For example, in *Art and Scholasticism* he cites Baudelaire almost as often as Aristotle and Aquinas. And it is significant that a great many of the Baudelaire quotations found in Maritain's work are taken from the aesthetics and criticism of the *poète maudit.* Baudelaire is apparently as important to Maritain in his role of critic as in his role of poet.

Baudelaire is for Maritain the one poet whose work is the most important for an understanding of the deepest tendencies of modern literature. He represents the inauguration of a modern movement that has sought to return art to its essential spirituality: a movement continued in this century by Picasso and the Cubists in painting and by Cocteau and Surrealism in poetry. The greatness of Baudelaire, says Maritain, is not to be seen in some revolution in poetic form or language. It lies rather in the extraordinary intensity of his poetic intuition. Thanks to this inner concentration of his poetic experience, the spiritual quality of the life of the senses reveals itself with rare brilliance and clarity in *Les Fleurs du mal (The Flowers of Evil).*

Baudelaire played a central role in revealing to modern poetry its essential spirituality. He abandoned himself to the supreme idol of beauty with a reckless disregard for the place of beauty's origin—whether it be heaven or hell ("Que tu viennes du ciel ou de l'enfer, qu'importe," Baudelaire, "Hymne à la Beauté"). The poetic heritage that he left for the modern artist was thus a spirituality that was profoundly ambivalent. The quest for the idol of beauty as separate from divine transcendence led Mallarmé and Valéry to the experience of the void. It led D. H. Lawrence to seek "mystical fusion with the demonism of Nature" (CI, 179), and Lautréamont to the experience of revolt. On the other hand, such poets as Hopkins, Eliot, Claudel, and Péguy were led to experience God's presence and "a contemplative knowledge of the soul and the world" (CI, 181). The most striking indication of the deep ambivalence of this spiritual heritage in modern poetry is that both Claudel and André Breton found their greatest inspiration and example in the very same Arthur Rimbaud.

IX *Surrealism*

Some of Maritain's very best literary criticism concerns the Surrealist experiment in modern poetry, which represents one of the principal directions in which Baudelaire's poetic heirs developed. Maritain is correct in saying that the whole origin of the Surrealist experiment was the poetic experience of Rimbaud, the *voyant,* who diverted poetry from its proper end beyond ends, or beauty, in order to concentrate exclusively on spiritual experience. Rimbaud attempted a violent abduction of spiritual experience in poetry for nonpoetic purposes. He sought to transform poetic knowledge into an absolute, magical knowledge. Instead of aiming for the creation of the work, poetry is now used for an unnatural end, to reveal absolute knowledge. It seeks to know, rather than to make. Magical knowledge, then, usurps the place of the idol beauty, and is identified with power. "Thus the achievement of a work, which is the genuine glory of the artist, is replaced by the quest for the human subject's omnipotence. And the delectation that beauty gives is replaced by the delight of experience of supreme freedom in the night of subjectivity" (CI, 188 - 89). Oscar Wilde had made life a means of poetry. Rimbaud and the Surrealists attempted to make poetry a means of life by forcing poetry out of the realm of art and into the sphere of morality.

Since the Surrealists thus make poetry subservient to the realization of absolute liberation and power, they naturally make an important distinction between the imagination and intellect. The primitive power of the automatic unconscious is for them a more important faculty, which should be cultivated to the exclusion of the intellect. Here Maritain catches Breton and his followers in an important contradiction. For whenever André Breton or another Surrealist produces a poem, the powers of the intelligence are involved; the very existence of Surrealist works gives the lie to their doctrine.

In their repudiation of beauty, says Maritain, the Surrealists were precursors of the dehumanization of modern culture through the influence of technology. Their poetic experiment is analogous to "a kind of asceticism at the service of the useful" (CI, 190). The absence of aesthetically pleasing architecture, art, or literature in the technocratic wasteland was prophesied in the Surrealists' dismissal of beauty for the sake of magical knowledge. For this reason Maritain suggests that art has an important mission. "It is the most natural power of healing and agent of spiritualization needed by the human community" (CI, 191).

In spite of the fact that Maritain spends a great deal of time analyzing the errors of Surrealism, he also confesses a genuine respect for the spiritual quality of the movement. The Surrealists were right to reemphasize the importance to the poet of the irrational, of chance, of psychic automatism. But this interest in the importance of madness in the poet was a dangerous development. Baudelaire, Rimbaud, Lautréamont, and the Surrealists were all involved in pushing poetry into new spiritual frontiers, regions where "the battle is waged between the good and the bad angels, and the bad angels are disguised as messengers of light" (AS, 130). And for Maritain it is Rimbaud's angelism that remains the classic example of the error of Surrealism, the tendency to expect from poetry the revelation of the all-saving absolute. The error of Surrealism teaches us that the poet is not the Messiah; he is the faithful craftsman.

X *The Modern Novel*

Two other recent trends in literature, especially in the field of the novel, have received particularly unfavorable comment from Maritain. The shift from the creative self to the self-centered ego whose origin he traces to the pernicious influence of Rousseau has led to a kind of "hero writer" in the modern age. Because of the aberration, the artist has become too preoccupied with the projection of his own image into the work. This trend has developed in two directions, which Maritain terms "emotionalism" and "shallow intellectualism." The contemporary literary heir to Rousseau, says Maritain, writes "for the therapeutic release of the repressed dreams and sex obsessions of his tormented reader or fostering, in the service of mankind and his ego together, that confusion of art and partisanship to which the *littérature engagée* seems committed." (CI, 194 - 95).

What, then, has Maritain to say of the other side of modern poetry's spiritual ambivalence? Of the poetry of Catholic writers —Claudel, Eliot, Mauriac, Bernanos, Green? His thinking on Christian art is especially cogent and sound. He is, as one would expect, a champion of Christian art. But for Maritain, Christian art is certainly not identifiable with "church art." He quotes Max Jacob's observation that "If Jammes and Claudel are Christian artists, it is not because of their manifest and distinctive devotion. The apostolate is never an aesthetic virtue" (AS, 96). Christian art is that which proceeds freely, without constraint, from the creativity of redeemed humanity. Above all, it is not the work of one who strives to produce an expressly Christian work.

This unique perspective on modern literature has produced some strikingly original and luminous commentaries on certain novelists of contemporary importance. Two of Maritain's memorable aphoristic criticisms concern Marcel Proust and Georges Bernanos. In *The Responsibility of the Artist,* he speaks of the material of the novelist as sin and discusses the dangerous necessity of immersion (if only imaginative) of the writer in this material in order to convey an authentic picture of a fictional character. The answer to the dilemma, suggests Maritain, is for the novelist to love his characters with a redeeming love, following the example of Bernanos, who, it is said, could not help praying for his own fictional characters! Again on the subject of the moral risks entailed in the modern novelist's descent into human misery, Maritain comments: "To write Proust's work as it needed to be written would have required the inner light of a Saint Augustine" (AS, 221). These are two examples of how in one statement Maritain is able to sum up so much of the art of a great novelist.

In his *Réponse à Jean Cocteau (Art and Faith),* Maritain has left some useful critical commentaries on the significance of Cocteau's work. The style in which this letter was written has a poetic quality that is unrivaled in the works of Maritain. He seems to have been especially conscious of the public for which he was writing, for this text, even more so than *Art and Scholasticism,* was to reach a wide variety of literary circles in France and elsewhere. Speaking of the importance of angels in Cocteau's work, he writes in the following passage with a luminous style reminiscent of the writings of Cocteau himself:

You would see them in window pane reflections, in the sensitive mirror of analogy, in enigmas, diagrams and rebuses; in poetry you were gradually rediscovering them, you were sensing their immensity, their strength, their tenderness, their elegance, their danger. For, to tell the truth, it was they who were catching you in a trap, holding the birdcatcher in their nets.[7]

Maritain praised Cocteau for the spiritualizing influence he had on modern poetry. He saw in Cocteau's "aesthetics of the tight rope" the same laws of purification and simplification *(dépouillement)* on which the scholastic theory of art is based.

The writings of André Gide have had a special appeal for the modern public, especially among the youth. Because of the great influence of this writer, Maritain has returned again and again to the problems posed by Gide, particularly concerning the relationship of art and morality. Extending the tendencies already implicit in his Symbolist literary heritage, Gide insisted that morality for him was a branch of aesthetics and that in order to insure the spontaneity of his work, the artist must be able to believe that it doesn't matter what one writes. What Gide was forgetting here, suggests Maritain, is that art and morality are autonomous realms, but they do coexist within the artist as a human being. Gide's error, he says, is a sin against the human subject of art. To eliminate all human ends to be followed in art is to be afraid of morality and to refuse one's humanity with all the thoughts and aspirations that make up one's personality.

Indeed, André Gide himself seems to have disregarded the necessity to believe that what one writes does not matter. In his own writings he most often seems motivated by what Maritain calls "a kind of apostolic zeal . . . the chief intent of which was to justify himself in the eyes of men" (RA, 56). This is the strategy at the basis of Gide's famous sincerity, a specious kind of honesty, according to Maritain, which might be termed defensive sincerity. "It consists not in *seeing* oneself, but in *accepting* or cherishing oneself at each moment as one is, and refusing to make any choice or moral decision" (RA, 95; Maritain's italics). The work of art becomes a kind of self-epiphany, and everything must be subordinated to the absolute free development of the self-centered ego that is to be manifested in it.

In *Art and Poetry,* Maritain takes issue with Gide on the proper interpretation of a novelist who was a great favorite to them both, Dostoevski. He argues that Gide feels so strong a kinship with Dostoevski that he projects many of his own feelings and attitudes on him. Warning against taking an excessively Gidean view of Dostoevski, Maritain alludes to Gide's famous story, *The Return of the Prodigal Son:* "Dostoevski never sent his younger brother to seek freedom in sin more daringly than he had done himself. He loved his brother too much, he had made his own voyage with too much sagacity, he knew too well what sin is."[8]

Maritain thus draws some fundamental distinctions between the moral proclivities of Gide's art and those of Dostoevski's. He also attacks Gide's tendency to interpret the ideologies of certain characters in Dostoevski's fiction as the writer's own. In this connection, he emphasizes the objective quality of Dostoevski's fiction. In the character, for example, of Kirilov, Dostoevski was depicting the wounds of the human race, not his own particular ones. He described them with deep compassion and understanding, and yet he did not present them as examples of health.

In this discussion Maritain is developing ideas that have greater applicability than just the fiction of Dostoevski or Gide. He is embarking upon the whole theory of the novel, to which he has made some very significant contributions throughout his critical writings. It will be remembered that Maritain finds the three moments of epiphany of the creative intuition in the poetic sense, the theme or action, and the number or harmonic expansion. These three epiphanies correspond respectively to the three major forms of the work of words: the poem or song, the drama, and the novel. The poetic space in the poetry of the novel is filled with the interrelationships of the characters, who are free and moral agents, autonomous human beings. This is the meaning of harmonic expansion.

Because the soul of the novel, so to speak, consists in the filling of its poetic space with subjectivities outside the artist's own self, it requires a special depth of poetic intuition. It is in this aspect of his art that the novelist proves his unique genius:

His work is similar to the living universe, there is in it a sort of *metaphysical pathos* because the beings who move about in it are, to a certain degree, in the same relation to the thought that creates them, as men are to God. He loves his characters, more tenderly perhaps than does any other artist, he puts himself into them more than does any other; at the same time, he scrutinizes them and judges them inflexibly.   (AP, 59)

In contrast to the dramatist, the novelist is concerned primarily with the free agents who carry out the action, rather than the action itself. In fact, the characters themselves often have as significant a role as the novelist in determining the direction the action will take. The distinctive function of the novelist, then, is to create humanity itself: "humanity to be formed, scrutinized and governed like a world" (AS, 221). And using the words of François Mauriac, Maritain adds that the "aim of the novel is knowledge of the human heart" (CI, 397).

XI *The Critic and Society*

Maritain's criticism offers an original conception of the critic and his proper role in society. Baudelaire, he observes, was of the opinion that great poets always possess the gifts of a critic but that a critic could never become a poet. Maritain modifies this concept by insisting that the gift of poetry inhabits both the poet and the critic. On one hand, poets are incomplete without a measure of the reflective intelligence that is more recognizable in critics (since poetry is a virtue of the practical intellect). Likewise, the critic must be capable of sharing the poet's intuitive experience of poetic knowledge if he is to judge the work with authority and sympathetic insight. "The critic must perceive much more purely and deeply than the ordinary reader all that which, conveyed by the poem, makes contact intuitively with the creative intuition of the poet. In other words, the critic is a poet, and has the gifts of a poet, at least virtually" (CI, 324).

The literary critic, then, in Maritain's view, is a creative writer in an alternative function, so that "in criticism we have art itself freely and rationally discussing and regulating art" (RA, 84). The phrase "discussing and regulating" in this passage sums up Maritain's idea of the critic's function in society. His responsibility is essentially twofold. First, he must be able to lead his public to a fuller appreciation of the work and its intrinsic artistic worth. How nearly does it realize the ideals of its particular craft, and for what reasons? But equally as important, he must judge the moral impact that the work may have on the human community as a whole. In other words, the critic does not remain within the sphere of making, in which art is the intellectual virtue to be judged. He also has the responsibility to place himself in the sphere of doing, in order to judge the work by the intellectual virtue of prudence.

This kind of global perspective on the interrelated responsibilities of artist, critic, and public in the world of art is an excellent example of the value of Maritain's philosophy. His writings in aesthestics and criticism are a unique and rich resource for students and teachers of art and literature, especially for those who have begun to confront the profound moral problems raised in the arts during the modern age.

CHAPTER 9

Aggiornamento *and*
The Peasant of the Garonne

I *A Stormy Reception*

THE last great controversy of Maritain's career was occasioned by the publication in 1966 of *The Peasant of the Garonne*.[1] By the 1960s, Maritain had firmly established a reputation among Catholic intellectuals, but that reputation was not without deceptive ironies. His repeated efforts to reveal the urgency of the church's temporal mission had earned him the overly simplistic label of a liberal. His "liberalizing" influence on the church had led to his being associated with people like Gabriel Marcel as a driving force behind the reforms of the Second Vatican Council. A great many Catholic intellectuals, who had considered Maritain as a kind of modern prophet, were scandalized when they found him hurling invectives against "neo-modernism," fresh on the heels of Vatican II. They felt almost betrayed. Where was the tactful, diplomatic Thomist whose intellectual courtesy had become a trademark? Catholic periodicals bristled with reviews and articles in which disenchanted Maritain admirers attempted to explain why their champion had turned reactionary.

There were two principal sources for the confusion that greeted *The Peasant of the Garonne*. First, Maritain had indeed allowed his fabled intellectual courtesy to lapse. The tone of the book is not characteristic of the bulk of his writings. Perhaps, at age eighty-five, he felt he deserved to be indulged in a bit of righteous indignation. His intimates, at any rate, insist that he had always been capable of rather animated demonstrations when his dearest convictions were in question, and that his gentleness was only a result of self-discipline and patience. The title of the book itself serves notice of this rather abrupt tone. A peasant of the Danube, according to La Fontaine, was someone who called a spade a spade. Maritain, since he was living with

126

the Little Brothers of Jesus near the Garonne River, simply appropriated the title for his own purposes.

The second reason for the widespread misunderstanding of *The Peasant of the Garonne* was the "liberal" label indiscriminately associated with its author. Too many people were unable to reconcile for themselves his political liberalism and his theological, or doctrinal, conservatism. In discussing the meaning of the often confusing terms "left" and "right," Maritain says: "I keep myself as far from both camps, but it is quite natural (if hardly pleasing) that I feel myself less distant from the first (left) when it is a question of things that are Caesar's, and less distant from the second alas! (right) when it is a question of the things that are God's" (PG, 26). When one finds himself in the political left, there is no reason for people to expect his religious thought to fit also the left end of the spectrum. The very basis for Maritain's social and political activism lay in the speculative philosophy, and notably the metaphysics, of Aristotle and Aquinas. Contrary to the mass of scandalized reviews, Maritain had not made a *volte-face*. His ideology in *The Peasant of the Garonne* is entirely consistent with his earlier works. The greatest shift is a superficial one concerned mainly with style and tone.

Maritain must have been well aware of the consternation among his readers that the return to his more aggressive, prophetic vein of *Antimoderne* had generated. He had offered *The Peasant of the Garonne* as his last book, and yet only a few years later (1970) he published *On the Church of Christ,* a book that delineates in greater detail some of the philosophical distinctions at the heart of the controversy of *The Peasant of the Garonne.* Notably, the tone of the 1970 publication is more characteristically tactful, less harsh than its immediate predecessor. It is, in great part, a sequel to Maritain's first public response to Vatican II and a continuation of his meditation on the whole movement of *aggiornamento.*

II *Antimodernism Revisited*

The most frequent targets of Maritain's wrath in *The Peasant of the Garonne* are the new wave of liberal theologians, the phenomenologists, the existentialists, the Freudians, the more extreme ecumenists, and especially the Teilhardians. In all of these currents of modernism, he sees a diluting of eternal truths, a watering down of immutable doctrine. The secularization of religious belief is epitomized for him in a book by an Anglican bishop that enjoyed a high degree of popularity among Christian laymen and theologians of the 1960s. In a sort of layman's version of Rudolf Bultmann's program of demythologizing, John A. T. Robinson's *Honest to God* offered what he called a "religionless Christianity." Bishop Robinson was concerned about the many doubting Christians of his time, and he was "so totally disheartened by the religious indifference of his contemporaries that in his struggle to help them he accommodates divine things in a way that will become acceptable to them and will at least awaken their appetite" (PG, 10). Theological modernism is a pernicious "chronolatry," or an epistemological adoration of time, fashion, trends. Such adaptation of eternal truths to trends of the moment is destructive of the very foundation of the Christian faith.

Maritain's ill-understood reaction to the modernists' perversion of Vatican II might have been more readily accepted, even anticipated, if his readers had paid closer attention to the concept of the ambivalence of the world, which he had already delineated in *Integral Humanism* and *On the Philosophy of History*. In a chapter entitled "The World and Its Contrasting Aspects," he once again returns to a biblically based understanding of the significance of the world for Christian philosophy and deepens its implications in the context of the world of 1966. The Christian must be aware that the world is saved, that God loved the world enough to send His Son to save it. Christ died for the whole world. Still he must also remember that the world is not holy or sacred; it stands in perpetual need of regeneration, for "the world was made by him, and the world did not know him" (John 10:11). Insofar as the world, then, rejected Christ and could not, as St. Paul says, comprehend the things of the spirit, it stands condemned.

According to Maritain, the Christian is called to a temporal mission. He is to involve himself in the temporal problems of his day. But the temporal mission of the Christian is like Ecclesiastes' "vanity and a striving after wind" without a firm spiritual underpinning. The primacy of the spiritual vocation in order to orient one's temporal involvement is the basic truth in which he remained unwaveringly consistent throughout his career. That, above all, is the paradox that seemed to fall on heedless ears during the controversy over *The Peasant of the Garonne.*

The modernists, says Maritain, have overreacted to a prejudice among Christians that goes back to the nineteenth century. That aberrant concept of the world held that is was too polluted with sin to be the direct concern of the Christian and that "the call to the perfection of charity . . . was the exclusive concern of the monks" (PG, 49). The pendulum, once set in motion by Vatican II in the opposite direction, was unable to control itself, and many modernists adopted a posture that Maritain terms "kneeling before the world." The new theologians, he observes, avoid speaking of such unpopular things as the other world, the cross, or sanctity. Their temporalization of Christian belief runs counter to the necessity for sanctity. For Maritain, the Christian is only enabled to ransom the time by dying to the world, like the saints, by holding the world in contempt for the sake of Christ. Only through that dark night of the soul can one begin to love the world with the redeeming love of Christ.

Maritain insists that while the Second Vatican Council was indeed the announcement of a new age, of a new call for Christians to embrace their temporal mission, it was not an adaptation of the church to the world. It was, instead, a reaffirmation of the church's perennial doctrine of the world, a doctrine that had been misinterpreted for too long. It was the kindling of a "true new fire," a new "epiphany of evangelical love," a love of non-Christians for what they are, and not just as souls to be converted. But in opening themselves to this new fire and in cooperating more freely with non-Christians for the achievement of common practical goals, Christians cannot permit fraternization to water down their doctrinal differences.

The more a Christian, or a Catholic, gives an absolute primacy in his heart to a fully liberated brotherly love, and in dealing with non-Catholics or non-Christians, sees them as they really are, members of Christ, at least potentially, the more firmly he must maintain his positions in the doctrinal order. . . . We must have a tough mind and a tender heart. (PG, 80)

In the fraternal dialogue of modern society, truth and charity must go hand in hand: charity for persons, truth for ideas. One sees a trace of Molière's misanthrope, Alceste, in Maritain's refusal to allow the demands of charity (for Alceste it would have been politeness) to becloud one's adherence to a faith to live by. "Let us beware of those brotherly dialogues in which everyone is in raptures while listening to heresies, stuff and nonsense of the other. They are not brotherly at all. It has never been recommended to confuse 'loving' with 'seeking to please' " (PG, 91). For Maritain, the contemporary equivalents to Molière's *petits marquis,* so smitten with politeness and affectation, are the fanatical ecumenists, who seek indiscriminate fraternization with the non-Christian at the expense of faithfulness to the truth.

Thomist philosophy, he suggests, has an especially crucial role to play in the authentic, legitimate dialogue between Christian and non-Christian. Philosophy is better equipped for such dialogue than theology, since it remains in the natural order and does not depend on revelation. It can work best toward an atmosphere that fosters a "natural ecumenism": an inborn desire for intellectual exchange and honest exploration of grounds of common agreement.

Maritain believes that in the crisis of modern civilization that forms the backdrop of *The Peasant of the Garonne,* the mission of Christian philosophy was vitally important. He seeks to put Christian philosophy into its perspective for modern man by comparing it with its rival systems of thought. First, he maintains that Marxist realism and Christian realism are the only two doctrines of modern times that can be properly called philosophical doctrines. Phenomenology, existentialism, and all the other modern descendants of Descartes's idealism, he says, are victims of the "Husserlian Parenthesis." This extension of Cartesian epistemology proclaims that being is "something that is *thought,* not something that *is*" (PG, 106; Maritain's italics). All such forms of idealism are thus what Maritain calls ideosophies, rather than philosophies. They make man "the measure of all things, even of the God he worships" (PG, 107).

As for the Marxist version of realism, it goes astray in identifying extramental reality with matter, thus reducing the spiritual to nothing more than a reflection of matter. Philosophy can profit from this immanentism, and therein lies the contribution that Sartrian existentialism has made to philosophy. But the philosopher of integral realism must make a critical examination of it, saving the authentic truths to which it points while winnowing out the errors in which it is involved. The intuition of metaphysical being is the antidote for all the dangerous errors of modern philosophy. If it is missing, the void that it leaves will necessarily be occupied by a pathological craving for fables and counterfeit intellectual currency. Julian Huxley, for example, attempted to use scientific concepts outside the proper sphere of science and ended up fabricating a pseudo-philosophical myth of the world.

III   The Teilhardian Tide

The best known and most controversial counterfeit intellectual currency that Maritain attacks in *The Peasant of the Garonne* is the Teilhardian system. Father Pierre Teilhard de Chardin was a Jesuit priest whose scientific research in the fields of paleontology and evolution, combined with his own unique personal faith, resulted in a theory of progressive incarnation that astounded scientists and theologians alike. Acclaimed by many as a great prophet, Teilhard expressed his visions of a new Christ and a new cosmos in lyrical outpourings that won many a convert to his novel ideas.

Maritain's treatment of what he considered dangerous philosophical errors in the doctrine of Teilhard is reminiscent of his treatment of Bergson and his philosophy. In both cases, he tries to maintain an attitude of charity toward the thinker and one of concern for truth toward the system of thought. According to Maritain, Teilhard was a great Christian and a great poet, but his philosophical and theological doctrines were misguided, and his admirers have even further perverted them. Etienne Gilson contends that Teilhard himself never really even conceived of his theories as doctrines, properly speaking, and never had any intention of spreading them.

Maritain is careful to point to the essential truth of Teilhard's message. "At the very root of Teilhard's thought there was, I believe, a poetic intuition—extremely powerful—of the sacred worth of created nature" (PG, 118). He compares Father Teilhard to a kind of Christian Lucretius. But in his "purely evolutive conception where being is replaced by becoming" (PG, 122), Teilhard sees the movement of history, scientifically and spiritually explained, as an evolution toward the "panchristizing" of the universe. The cosmos becomes perfected in its progressive identification with Christ. Science thus enjoys a dazzling primacy in this doctrine, which Maritain terms a

Christian gnosis. The fundamental error in this philosophy, he says, is that "science, faith, mystique, theology and philosophy in a diffused state, are inextricably mingled and confounded" (PG, 119). Such an indiscriminate mingling of the degrees of knowledge is obviously a cardinal sin against the basic tenets of epistemology.

But in a critique that is reminiscent of his assessment of Bergsonism many years before, Maritain suggests that Teilhardism is most insidious in the form given to it by Teilhard's more fanatical disciples, who further perverted his systems after his death. "While it is true that *Teilhardism* . . . presents itself as a doctrine . . . what matters essentially in *Teilhard himself* is a personal experience, and truly speaking, incommunicable" (PG, 120; italics mine). "The religious experience of Père Teilhard actually counts for much more than his doctrine" (PG, 124).

In the 1920s Maritain saw what he considered a perilous philosophical error in a Bergsonism that, in the hands of Bergson's followers, was betraying the original intent of Bergson's own theories. In the 1960s he again saw a dangerous adaptation of a theoretical system. In both cases, he has scrupulously pointed out how the disciples have misused or twisted the original thrust of the theorist himself, and he has also taken care to identify the most valuable contributions that Bergson and Teilhard have made to humanity and to Christian culture.

IV *Thomas and the Thomists*

From his critique of Teilhardism, Maritain moves directly in *The Peasant of the Garonne* to a brief review of the importance of Thomas Aquinas, of his philosophy, and of the intuition of metaphysical being. The contrast is obvious and intentional: Maritain seeks to induce his reader to draw a comparison between the philosophical error of modernism and its most effective antidote. In beginning his discussion of Teilhard, he expresses amazement at the fact that despite Teilhard's sound training as a Jesuit, he seems to have remained untouched by the thought of Aquinas. In fact, one of the basic weaknesses in Teilhard's thought, he surmises, may possibly be attributed to his philosophical isolation, the fact that Father Teilhard seemed intent on working out his system in solitude, without the help of philosopher and theologian friends.

If, then, the corrective for modernist errors like Teilhard's lies in a sound Thomist intuition of metaphysical being, where does one go from here? Well, it is obvious even to the casual observer of contemporary philosophy that Thomism is not the most fashionable philosophy of our era. And yet Maritain here refrains from playing the Jeremiah and contends that the twentieth century has seen some rather significant progress by Thomist philosophers—especially in the fields of critique of Oriental thought and the theory of natural mysticism. Indeed, it must certainly be added that Maritain's own work, along with that of Etienne Gilson and others, has brought about a renewal of Thomist philosophy the likes of which had not been witnessed since John of Saint Thomas. The first priority among the urgent needs of the Thomist renewal, according to Maritain, is a thoroughgoing revision of the Thomist philosophy of nature. Obviously, such a project would go a long way toward clearing the air of the fallout that lingers from the Teilhardian explosion.

In order for Thomism to serve the function demanded of it in the contemporary cultural crisis, what should be its new direction? Some have suggested that theology today should do with the modern philosophies what Aquinas did with Aristotle. For Maritain, what actually lies concealed in this suggestion is the desire to have modern theologies use the philosophies of their age to reinterpret faith itself, to adapt the immutable things of faith to each new age.

While the object of theology continues to remain the truth of the mysteries of faith (but a truth henceforth mutable in its intelligible value and meaning, at times mythical if necessary)—and also, of course, the truths of erudition (absolute, these ones, if only for the moment) — nevertheless, the ultimate purpose of theology, finally, has become no longer Truth but Efficacy. (PG, 45)

And by subordinating truth to efficacy, philosophy throws off the role of handmaiden to theology and becomes instead her mistress.

What is really demanded of Thomist theology today, insists Maritain, is not to adapt itself to contemporary philosophies, but to bring to them the perspective of a higher wisdom, to enlighten and purify them, and to ransom the authentic truths they hold captive.

Thomism at its best has been a philosophy of realism because of its profound openness to the real. But after Saint Thomas, the increasing need for scholastic disputation to defend precious Thomist doctrines gradually led to a kind of intellectual sclerosis in modern Thomism. Thomists gradually lost their openness, and when modern science began to proclaim its great discoveries, Thomists replied only by way of refutation. Finally, by the time of Vatican II, Christian thought was ready to redress its intellectual sclerosis. But Maritain sees a grave danger in the momentum that the swinging pendulum seems inevitably to gain in such a transition. "When worm-eaten barriers begin to snap, a horde of bewildered souls are quick to take advantage of it and disperse in nature—or 'culture' and blithely follow the prevailing winds, in other words, the latest fashion" (PG, 152).

The frantic rush toward new cultural trends can result in an overbearing influence being accorded to disciplines that often sacrifice content for technique. This kind of superficial mentality favors psychology over wisdom, for example. Indeed, a noticeable trend among modernist clergymen and theologians is to rely more heavily on the promises of psychological technique than the power of the Holy Spirit. "Nothing will be achieved by an idiotic attempt to break everything in order to do up everything to the taste of the day; what is needed is an effort of the mind to see more deeply into the mystery which it will never finish probing" (PG, 160).

In pointing to the paucity of professors teaching in the name of the church who actually profess allegiance to St. Thomas's philosophy, Maritain suggests that the situation might be somewhat alleviated if the church changed its method of recommending Thomist doctrine. Traditionally, Canon Law had required professors who hold their function from the church to abide by the principles and teachings of Thomas Aquinas in the teaching of philosophy. Maritain speculates that better results might be accomplished "by appealing less to obedience and docility than to the freedom of the intellect in its pursuit of truth" (PG, 169). Such an approach is perhaps more consistent with the church's confidence in the Angelic Doctor's teachings.

V *The Church Today*

The final (and by far the longest) chapter of *The Peasant of the Garonne* concerns the doctrine and nature of the church and the respective roles of contemplative and liturgical life in the contemporary Christian's response to a world of great human need. It is a vast subject that Maritain knew he could not exhaust in a single chapter. In the years following the publication of *The Peasant of the Garonne,* he decided against his original intention to make it his last book and wrote a more detailed study of these same problems, *On the Church of Christ,* published in 1970.

The most far-reaching distinction stressed by Maritain in both these late works is the one expressed in the subtitle of the 1970 book: "The Person of the Church and Her Personnel." Contemporary critics—yea, even some reformers—of the church often fail to take this distinction into consideration. According to this doctrine, which is one of the mysteries of faith, "the Church herself is *without sin* because her own life is grace and charity" (CC, 11; Maritain's italics). Even at the historical moments when the church seemed to be at her nadir (the Inquisition, the worst of the Crusades, the trials of Joan of Arc and Galileo, etc.), the corruption of which she has been accused did not sully her divine person, but rather her human personnel. Insofar as a member of the church sins, he separates himself from the life of the church. "Composed of members who are all sinners, and who all bear in themselves the wounds of original sin, the Church herself, *holy and immaculate, without stain,* 'indefectibly holy', is pure of all trace of sin" (CC, 9; Maritain's italics).

Maritain adds that in order to understand the church in her wholeness *(intégralité),* one must think of the person of the church as composed of all souls in grace, whether they be in heaven, purgatory, or earth. There are infinitely more souls in the heavenly sojourn of the church. Therefore, when her earthly aspect appears lost, one is considering only a small part of the church. The heavenly aspect is constantly praying for her earthly sister, and it is in this sense that Maritain understands Christ's statement that the gates of hell will never prevail against the church.

In a similar sense, Maritain speaks of a distinction between the *visible* church and the *invisible* church. The former consists of the hierarchical structure, the liturgical rites, and the people who declare themselves formally to belong to the church. The latter is

the presence of divine grace, which can exist in human souls
without the trappings of ecclesiastical structure, rites, etc.
"Divine grace does not verify only the visible members of the
Church; it verifies also, in the entire world, an incalculable
number of men who are members of other spiritual families,—
religious or areligious,—and who sincerely seek God, even without knowing it themselves; they belong invisibly to the visible
Church" (CC, 77). Therefore, the age-old dictum according to
which there is no salvation outside the church does not apply to
those who are outside the visible church but belong invisibly to
her. And the "spiritual families," many of whose members
belong invisibly to the church of Christ, according to Maritain,
are of a surprising variety. He considers all major world religions
in this context and even points to the analogues of Christian
grace that are found characteristically in modern Marxism and
the hippie movement.

The Marxist's concern for the amelioration of an exploited
proletariat and his awareness of the dehumanizing potential of a
profit-oriented economy constitute "traces" of the church's
presence. Without amounting to efficacious means of salvation,
they are a purely temporal call to a more humanized social
condition.

Maritain's analysis of the hippie movement is most incisive.
He calls it a "worldwide phenomenon and one of great significance" and observes that its essence lies in a "refusal *en bloc* of
the lies of civilization" (CC, 125). Its most instructive aspect is
the judgment it brings on a modern culture built on hollow
values: money, science, power, etc. Indeed, there is a parallel
between the hippies' refusal of modern culture and the great
mystics' refusal of the world. But the analogy breaks down when
one looks at the motives behind the two refusals. In the case of
the Christian mystic, he refuses the world in favor of "a truth
infinitely superior to the world" (CC, 126), whereas the hippie's
refusal is nothing more than escapism. For Maritain, the hippies
are "the victims of this bourgeois world which they are right in
detesting. In their flight they carry all its misery with them"
(CC, 126). The object of their flight, then, is the opposite of the
bourgeois values: irrationality, hedonism, full liberation of the
senses. The most authentic values found in the hippie culture are
the occasional blossoming forth of natural poetry and what
Maritain calls a beautiful kind of "vegetable purity . . . an

ideal of *purity of nature,* of sincerity, of candid spontaneity" (CC, 127; Maritain's italics). Maritain expressed admiration for these values but he adds that most standards that arise from the hippie movement are "a general counterfeit of the values of the spirit" (CC, 127).

In an article in *Le Figaro littéraire*[2], Maritain displayed once again his incisive understanding of contemporary social movements, weighed with objectivity and compassion in the light of eternal truths. The 1968 student revolt was obviously another manifestation of many of the same problems that gave birth to the hippie movement. Despite the strident nihilist voices of some of the student leaders, who seemed lost in a mindless conformism to pseudo-marxism, the most profound source of the French youth's frustrations, said Maritain, was a metaphysical wound: a wound inflicted on the souls of young Frenchmen by an intelligentsia that had systematically deprived them of any *raison de vivre.* Thus, Maritain saw the events of May 1968, as a most timely alarm signal, another warning against the soulless civilization that would result if the technocratic trends in modern culture remained unchecked. He expressed great faith in the elite of French youth to have the discernment to search out the "true new fire" among their teachers and to struggle for truth. Such developments, he suggested, are the only hope for guiding modern culture toward a technology truly in the service of the good of humanity.

VI *Contemplation and Commitment*

In order to express in the most cogent terms possible what Maritain believed to be the new message of the Second Vatican Council, he chose to quote the words of his great Thomist friend, Cardinal Charles Journet, who wrote in *La Revue Thomiste:* "The Church turns toward her lay children with a concern, not so much to shield them from evil as to *send* them into the midst of dangers with God in their hearts, in order to give witness to the Gospel."[3] The contemporary Christian has an unprecedented clear call to fulfill the temporal mission of the church, but he must not attempt to answer that call without acknowledging the source of inner strength required to accomplish his mission. The great contemplative monastic orders have historically cut themselves off from the world in order to deepen their spiritual devotion. They too feel the urgency of renewal today, but the call to minister to the suffering of the world does not, for them, "pull down or crack the sacred walls which shield from the world their solitude" (PG, 195). Both the layman and the monk are called to minister to the world *and* to deepen their own prayer lives.

"What matters in a very special way, and perhaps more than anything else, for our age, is the life of prayer and of union with God lived *in the world*" (PG, 196 - 97; Maritain's italics). Gone are the days when an arbitrary dichotomy between man's religious and secular states fostered the belief that most people are called only "to live a good worldly life, not over-pious, and solidly planted in social naturalism" (PG, 197), while they leave it to the monasteries to win heaven for them. Christ's commandment in the Sermon on the Mount—"Be ye therefore perfect" (Matthew 5:48)—according to Maritain, is the guide for the "true new fire" in the church. All, he declares, are called to perfect charity, to the life of prayer and contemplation. And once more he reminds the modernists that the temporal mission is not to bring earth to perfection, in the sense of realizing the Kingdom of God in history. The temporal mission of the church, then, is more modest and realistic than that of communism, for example. But the fulfillment of that mission is the affair of the layman no less than the priest. All Christians are called to live the Gospel in whatever day-to-day circumstances in which they are involved.

By this summary of *The Peasant of the Garonne* and other writings of Maritain's postconciliar period, it is clear that much of the furor touched off by the book was baseless. Granted, the author's inability to conceal his distaste for certain alleged perversions of the spirit of Vatican II was largely responsible for the shocked reactions of Catholic liberals who had long admired Maritain. But at the same time, a great many of those aroused Catholics had not fully understood the paradoxical combination of liberal social theory and conservative theology in Maritain's work before that time. A careful, dispassionate analysis of *The Peasant of the Garonne* and *On the Church of Christ,* however, reveals his fundamental teachings in both the socio-political and theological realms to be entirely consistent with those of his earlier writings.

CHAPTER 10

Maritain and Literature

MARITAIN lived through all the crises, all the wars, and all the literary movements of our age, and in the course of his long life he made many friendships. In the world of art and letters he was to some an enthusiastic supporter, to others a close friend, and to many a compelling presence. But whether his influence was welcomed or repulsed, that strong presence always asserted itself and was felt by many a painter and poet. The fact that Maritain was one of the great contemplatives of our time was never able to keep him from taking a stand on an important issue, and it never prevented him from getting involved with artists and writers.

The relation and influence of Maritain to the literary and artistic world have received less attention than perhaps any other aspect of his work. And yet it is a concern that was very close to his heart. One of his favorite sayings of Saint Thomas is that man cannot live long without delectation, and the delectations offered in art, music, and literature were indeed vital to him. Moreover, in addition to his many friendships among men of letters, his wife Raïssa was a very sensitive poet herself and worked closely with him in aesthetics and criticism. Maritain's position in the modern world of letters is of undeniably great significance, especially in the context of the French Catholic literary renaissance in the first quarter of the century, of which he has been recognized as standard bearer. Beyond that, it would be difficult to assess just how great an influence he has exerted on writers who might not be associated with his religious views. But since the publication of *Creative Intuition in Art and Poetry* in 1953, his aesthetics and criticism have reached even further into the literary public at large.

139

I   *Early Influences and Associations: Psichari*

Ernest Psichari, the first great friend of Jacques Maritain's life, was to remain for him the most intimate and most cherished one, despite his early death in 1914. As earlier noted, the two youths first met at the Lycée Henri IV and went on to study together at the Sorbonne. The illustrious heritage they shared in the Favre and Renan families seems to have destined them for one another, although their spiritual itineraries were to prove ironic in the light of that heritage. Their works would one day represent an eloquent rejection of the agnostic positivism their famous forebears had stood for.

During their school days, Psichari, who was Maritain's junior by a year, was passionately devoted to him. The most significant event of this period in Psichari's life, however, was his unrequited passion for Jacques's older sister. When Jeanne Maritain, several years older than the impressionable student, told him she was not in love with him and already intended to marry someone else, Psichari made an unsuccessful suicide attempt. Then he fled his friends to live in depression and moral dissolution, until finally he found a form of salvation: He would enlist in the French Army and submit himself to its discipline.

While Psichari performed military duty in Africa, Maritain was constantly corresponding with him, telling him of his conversion and of his hope for Ernest to share the same joy with him. In the books he wrote during these years *(Voyage du Centurion, L'Appel des Armes,* etc.), Psichari chronicled his own spiritual development. And in his letters to his friend he revealed his attraction for "that beautiful spiritual home" held out to him by Maritain.

From the time of this letter in 1909, Psichari drew steadily closer to the faith in which he had been baptized as a child. Jacques's friendship was undoubtedly a decisive influence, and Ernest was confirmed and took his first communion in February 1913, during a visit with the Maritains in Versailles. It was only eighteen months before his death on the battlefield, where he was defending France from the invasion of 1914.

With Psichari—and most of the other names to be treated in this chapter—it was primarily Maritain's influence that exerted itself on his friend. But in the case of Péguy, Bergson, and Bloy, it was *their* influence on Maritain that was at least as important, and any discussion of Maritain's place in literature would be sadly inadequate without acknowledging his debt to these three writers, and theirs to him.

II *Péguy*

Charles Péguy was a rebellious young poet and polemicist when Maritain met him in 1901. He was in the process of launching the famous *Cahiers de la Quinzaine,* a literary journal that became the medium for disseminating all Péguy's ideas. These ideas were consistently atheist and socialist at the time, and much of the content of the *Cahiers* was intended to arouse support for the oppressed, the poor, and victims of prejudice. Péguy had been a militant Dreyfusard, and in 1901 he was still fighting the injustice that had plagued his country during its great turn of the century *crise de conscience.* It was largely from Péguy, and from Raïssa Maritain, that Jacques learned his lessons in championing the cause of the persecuted Jewish race.[1]

Péguy and Maritain were extremely close during the latter's years at the Sorbonne, and it was Péguy who suggested that Maritain attend Bergson's lectures. Mme Geneviève Favre-Maritain was at this time accustomed to receive friends on Thursdays for lunch and intellectual discussion and debate. Eventually, Péguy, who had been brought by her son, became a more regular habitué of Mme Favre-Maritain's gatherings than Jacques himself. Maritain's mother became so attached to Péguy that she hoped her son would one day carry on the vocation of the older writer at the *Cahiers de la Quinzaine.*

In 1907, the Maritains' conversion was still unknown to all but a few of their friends. Jacques had come to Paris from Heidelberg for a brief visit that year, and when he revealed his secret to Péguy he was greeted by the happy exclamation: "I too have come to that!" This should have been the occasion for a deepening of Maritain's friendship with Péguy, but for numerous complicated reasons, it was the beginning of a grave falling out between the two.

Péguy's conversion was a delicate subject for him, and he was hesitant to break the news too suddenly to the subscribers of the *Cahiers de la Quinzaine,* whom he seems to have considered a faithful flock entrusted to him for guidance. To add to the sensitiveness of his position, his wife was an adamant atheist and absolutely refused to have their civil marriage regularized by the church or to have their children baptized. Ecclesiastical authorities forbade him to partake of the sacraments until he could prevail upon his wife. Maritain was unable to understand how Péguy could abstain so long from the sacraments and persistently urged him to be more forceful with Mme Péguy. Finally, Péguy asked his friend to intercede, and the result was an unfortunate argument between Maritain and Mme Péguy.

There were other misunderstandings and imprudent words between the two friends, largely centering on Péguy's refusal to satisfy the conditions for full reentry into the faith of his childhood and on his anticlericalism and anti-intellectualism. The crisis came to a head in 1912, when Péguy published Julien Benda's viciously anticlerical novel *L'Ordination* in the *Cahiers de la Quinzaine*. Maritain responded by returning his copy to Péguy with a note asking him not to send any more reading of that sort to him. Péguy retaliated by ordering Maritain's name stricken from the list of his subscribers, an action that amounted to a kind of excommunication. The break was now complete and remained so until shortly before the war.

The sequel, of course, was a happy one, in that a reconciliation took place in 1914, and not long afterward Péguy attended mass, his first in many years. After he died in the battle of the Marne, his long-suffering faith was rewarded by the conversion of his wife and children to the Catholic faith.[2] In *Adventures in Grace,* Raïssa Maritain takes care to make understood that despite their differences with Péguy, the Maritains never doubted his faith. She insists that it would be a mistake to cast him in the role of a rebel or an impenitent free thinker. He was, she writes, "a Catholic of deep faith, a man of prayer absorbed by the idea of the temporal task of the Christian."[3] From all accounts, it is likely that Maritain's acceptance of the Catholic faith was not without significance in the life of Péguy. Mme Maritain suggests that Péguy's response to Maritain's revelation in 1907 may have been "a premature fruit in Péguy's inner life," that in a moment of emotion at hearing of his friend's new faith, he may have forced, as it were, a development that was still at a very tentative stage within him. Certainly, Péguy left a lasting mark on the philosophy of Maritain, an influence that is evident in his social consciousness and his passion for justice.

III *Bergson*

One of the most important influences that Péguy exerted on Maritain was to introduce him to the thought of Henri Bergson. Bergson's philosophy had been a vitally formative force in Péguy's work, as indeed it was for the other great writers of the early twentieth century who ushered in an era of new creativity in French literature: Proust, Gide, Valéry, and Claudel. It was Bergson who saved Maritain from philosophical despair by offering him a viable alternative to the dead end of positivism. And although Maritain at once became an enthusiastic disciple of Bergson, his writings and lectures in the years just preceding the First World War were regarded as violently anti-Bergson. According to Raïssa Maritain, her husband's controversial work was actually aimed not so much at Bergsonism itself as against the dangerous misuse of pseudo-Bergsonism among young Catholics in which aimless sentimentality masqueraded as the Bergsonian doctrine of "intuition."

Nonetheless, the public interpreted the whole episode as a desertion by the upstart young philosopher of his former master. But as with Péguy, Bergson was not to remain forever alienated from his former pupil. By the end of his career, he had come to the point of accepting Catholicism,[4] although he refused baptism out of concern for the persecution of his own Jewish race. In the late 1930s, Raïssa Maritain visited him and found that all the differences of the past had been forgotten. Her aging master told her that Jacques had been right in his critique of Bergsonism as a system over against Bergsonism of intention. "Since then," he added, "we have moved toward each other, and we have met in the middle of the way."[5]

IV *Bloy*

The last and most important member of the trio of early acquaintances who were formative influences on the young Maritain was Léon Bloy. Like Péguy, Bloy was a zealous defender of the poor, and he shared their lot.[6] When Maritain met him in 1905, he noticed that his corduroy jacket was buttoned all the way to his neck. In time he realized that there was no shirt under it—Bloy was literally too poor to buy a shirt.

Léon Bloy's influence on Maritain was deeper and more lasting than any of his other early associations, first as a uniquely devout Christian but also as a writer and thinker. Some of Maritain's more striking theological ideas are extensions of Bloy's thought—for example, the notion that the saints in heaven, and even God himself, actually suffer for men in earthly life. Maritain also spent two years doing a study—which has remained unpublished—of the appearance of the Holy Virgin to a shepherdess at La Salette, a devotion that was especially dear to Bloy. And although the tone of most of Maritain's works is characteristic of a man of great gentleness and intellectual courtesy, he was known in the beginning of his career as a writer with an inflammatory, prophetic style whose intractable fidelity to the scholastic method was the cause of frequent controversy. This stubborn prophetic quality—which recurred more recently in *The Peasant of the Garonne*—is another example of Bloy's profound influence.

V *Rouault*

There is one final relationship of Maritain's early years that had an important effect on his writing. He had met the painter Georges Rouault at Bloy's house in 1905, but the two were never close until the Maritains' residence at Versailles in 1909. Rouault lived in the neighborhood and soon began to have dinner with them regularly. It was a time of deep crisis for Rouault, whose struggle to express his own revolutionary creativity was being met on all sides with misunderstanding and scorn. Even Bloy, who had had his mark on Rouault, too, was hostile to the painter's somber style of this period. But in Jacques and Raïssa Maritain, Rouault found encouragement, sympathy, and understanding.

The Maritains were thus privileged to be the intimate witnesses of a heroic struggle in modern art. Rouault was for them the existential revelation of a true Christian artist. "It was in the concrete example he furnished that we first perceived the nature of art, its imperious necessities, its antinomies and the very real and sometimes tragic conflict between opposed duties for which the mind of the artist can be the battleground."[7]

It was through his acquaintance with Rouault that Maritain learned of the vital difficulties of the artist's life and especially of the heroic fidelity that a great artist must maintain with regard to his inner conception of art. These ideas are among the most eloquently expressed ones in Maritain's aesthetics, and he has repeatedly said that he wrote *Art and Scholasticism* with Rouault primarily in mind. By the same token, the encouragement and sympathy that Rouault found at the Maritain home were an important consolation during the time of his most difficult trials.

VI *Thomist Gatherings at Meudon: Three Philosophers*

The years at Meudon were those in which Maritain's influence on the French literary world was at its zenith. The complete list of those who visited 10, rue du Parc would be a "Who's Who" of modern French letters. For Maritain's importance at this time, as it has been throughout his career, could not be confined to philosophers and clerics. During this same period, the Russian Orthodox philosopher Nicolai Berdiaev was accustomed to receiving guests in much the same manner as the Maritains. In fact, the two philosophers often exchanged visits themselves and found that they shared a great many ideas. Their philosophical disagreements—which often developed into heated debates that must have been fascinating to witness—centered on Berdiaev's mystical concept of knowledge as a gnosis, which was in direct conflict with Maritain's fundamental intellectualism. It was an inevitable opposition implicit in the meeting of Russian Orthodox mystical tradition with the Thomist-Aristotelian tradition of respect for the intellect represented by the two philosophers. But their thinking was in close agreement in regard to the ideal of a humanist and personalist social order.[8]

It was not uncommon to find many of the Meudon habitués at Berdiaev's gatherings at Clamart. One example was Etienne Gilson, who is well-known both in France and North America for his important work on the history of scholastic thought. Gilson was a young Thomist himself, and yet in his book *Le Thomisme* (1922), he had expressed some grave doubts of the proper role of faith in the philosophical sphere. On one particular occasion when Berdiaev took issue with Maritain on the same subject, he turned to Gilson for added support. But to everyone's surprise, Gilson replied that his views on faith and reason had come to coincide exactly with Maritain's. Recounting the episode in his diary, Maritain said he was touched by Gilson's intellectual candor, and the experience marked the beginning of his friendship with Gilson.

Another Catholic philosopher who was an occasional visitor at Meudon was Gabriel Marcel—like Maritain a convert to Catholicism who had rebeled against positivism and had been deeply influenced by Henri Bergson. These two philosophers had basic differences of temperament, and, as Henri Bars has observed, Marcel had his left where Maritain had his right and vice versa.[9] But they were together in 1934 in signing the manifesto "Pour le bien commun," and they were both influential in bringing about the liberalizing movement of the church leading up to Vatican II.[10]

VII   *Three Great Writers*

One of the most widely known and respected figures of the French Catholic literary renaissance was Paul Claudel, who not only wrote poetry and plays of lasting importance, but also served his country as ambassador to the United States and to China among other countries. It is interesting to note that Claudel's and Maritain's conversions came from distinct and independent literary sources, which may be represented by the following diagram:

I.	Barbey d'Aurévilly		
	Ernest Hello	Léon Bloy	
			Jacques Maritain
	Saint Geneviève		
	Henri Bergson	Charles Péguy	
	Joan of Arc		
II.	Arthur Rimbaud	Paul Claudel	Jacques Rivière
	Lautréamont		Francis Jammes

Many of the other conversions in French literary circles near the turn of the century can be situated somewhere within this schematic representation.

Although Claudel was not a regular attendant of the Thomist meetings at Meudon, he was seen there from time to time. There were some rather serious disagreements between Maritain and

Claudel on political issues, such as the Spanish Civil War; Claudel usually found the philosopher's political views too liberal. But they collaborated on projects such as the Dominican weekly *Sept,* and Maritain has felt compatible enough with Claudel's ideas to quote him often and to praise him highly in his critical commentaries. In her diary, Raïssa described him as a true Christian with a strong soul and a bizarre personality. But the Maritains were conscious of the great beauty of Claudel's poetry and held him in high esteem.

Maritain's relationship with Jean Cocteau is one of the most dramatic stories that occurred during the Meudon years. Cocteau was known as the young prodigy of French poetry, the dazzlingly inventive "enfant terrible" of his time. But the sudden death in 1923 of his friend and companion the young poet Raymond Radiguet had left him disconsolate. In his despair Cocteau had become addicted to opium and had come close to committing suicide. Max Jacob and Maritain were two friends who were especially helpful in seeing him through the darkest moments of the *désintoxication,* the drying out period that finally cured his addiction.

At the time of his cure, Cocteau had been told that Maritain was the man best suited to bringing him spiritual comfort, and so the poet decided to visit Meudon. During one of these visits, Cocteau met Father Charles Henrion, a member of the Little Brothers of Jesus, who had devoted his life to ascetic contemplation and service in the deserts of Africa. Cocteau was so overwhelmed by this example of a man chosen by God that he later asked Father Charles to confess him and took communion in the private chapel that was housed in the Maritain villa at Meudon. "A priest struck me with the same shock as Stravinsky and Picasso" (AF, 41), wrote Cocteau. For him it was a long-awaited return to his childhood faith, and in his *Lettre à Jacques Maritain* he wrote of his renewed zeal: "I should like intelligence to be taken away from the devil and returned to God. . . . Art for art's sake, or for the people are equally absurd. I propose art for God" (AF, 46, 55).

Cocteau's devotion to the church was, however, not destined to last. And "art for God," moreover, was not what Maritain had in mind himself, as he pointed out in his reply to Cocteau: "God does not ask for 'religious art' or 'catholic art.' The art He wants for Himself is art. With all its teeth" (AF, 91). Writing in

La Revue de Paris in 1953, Cocteau reminisced on the subject of the men who had most influenced his life, one of whom was "that admirable soul of Maritain." He explained that his *Lettre à Jacques Maritain* had been misunderstood and for that reason he had resolved to return to his "combative solitude, retaining my respect and my tenderness for Maritain, which I shall keep all my life."[11]

André Gide was a third great writer who was influenced by Maritain, but he resisted that influence more tenaciously than the others we have mentioned. During the Catholic literary renaissance, a great number of Gide's literary freinds were converted or reconverted to Catholicism: Henri Ghéon, Francis Jammes, Jacques Copeau, Jacques Rivière, Gabriel Marcel, and Julien Green are a few mentioned by Mme Raïssa Maritain in this context. It was no secret that the growing number of Catholic writers were eager to enroll André Gide's name on their list, and their attempts to bring him into the fold were persistent. Gide, however, regarded these attempts with bemused disdain. He referred to them as "flirtations."

There were two especially memorable meetings of André Gide and Jacques Maritain, each occasioned by controversial moments in Gide's career. In 1920, Gide had finished writing his first really explicit book on homosexuality, *Corydon,* in which he openly avowed his own experience and gave a passionate defense of homosexuality. It was known in 1923 that Gide was planning to publish the work, but the Catholic writers were hopeful of dissuading him. The task of convincing Gide of the book's potentially destructive influence was a particularly difficult one. It could not be a flattering role for one to accept, but Maritain agreed to try.

The account of this visit that Gide gives in his *Journal* is one of two great duellers carefully searching for a weakness to attack. These men represented two rival movements of contemporary literature, and they were aware of the causes they were defending. But it is also the moving story of two great souls who tried to reach out to each other. Maritain once told Julien Green that Gide's account of the incident had failed to mention that Gide had shown Maritain the letters he had received from Claudel and that in showing them to him he was moved to tears. From the outset, Gide felt unable to play any roles before Maritain. The two spoke slowly but frankly of their contrasting versions of

Christian faith. In the end, Gide remained unshakable, and Maritain left in disappointment.

The André Gide of the late 1920s and early 1930s was an increasingly political writer. His social consciousness had become more and more evident, and he openly expressed great hopes for society's salvation in the promises of the new Russia. The controversies triggered by this new convert to Communism were the subject of a colloquium sponsored by the "Union pour la vérité" on January 23, 1935. The participants included not only Gide and Maritain but such important figures as François Mauriac, Gabriel Marcel, Henri Massis, and Ramon Fernandez. It was a meeting surrounded by a theatrical atmosphere, one of those intellectual debates that have gained the notoriety of *"événements parisiens."*

The text of the meeting, published by the *Nouvelle Revue Française,* reveals Maritain's subtle but trenchant use of his philosophical training in the service of the faith. He began by calling Gide's conversion to Communism a moving act worthy of his respect. Then he analyzed what he felt were the elements that Communism shared with Christianity. For Maritain interpreted Gide's conversion to Communism as an attempt to realize values that are essentially evangelical. Communism, he warned, could not, however, remain a viable doctrine for a man like Gide, because it compromised the freedom of artistic creation, and, even more so, the freedom of the person. This warning proved prophetic, as Gide's travels in Russia only a year later disclosed to him the realities of the situation, which clashed with his own ideals. Finally, Maritain observed that Gide's reasons for adopting Communism would be considered rather *"petit bourgeois"* by orthodox Marxists. "To subscribe to a doctrine for reasons that it rejects seems to me a serious duality, and one about which a person so concerned as you are with sincerity could not but question himself."[12]

VIII *Among the Faithful*

During the Meudon years there were a number of writers who visited the Maritain villa with regularity and whose thinking was very closely associated with Maritain's. These members of a kind of inner circle of the faithful at Meudon were deeply influenced by Maritain in the realms of religion, art, and politics.

Some readers of Georges Bernanos will undoubtedly be surprised to find him listed "among the faithful," for relations between him and Maritain were often strained. But he was definitely closer to Maritain in all respects than were Claudel, Cocteau, or Gide. At the time of the publication of *The Star of Satan* (*Sous le soleil de Satan,* 1926), the two writers were beginning to develop a rich friendship. Bernanos felt so much respect for Maritain that he made certain changes in the manuscript on the philosopher's advice. For his part, Maritain admired the novel enough to use what influence he had with the Vatican officials in order to avert a papal censure of the controversial book, a possibility that had been rumored shortly after its publication.

These propitious beginnings of the Maritain-Bernanos acquaintance were dealt an almost lethal blow by the crisis of l'Action Française, to which they reacted in opposite fashion. Although the two were in essential agreement on the central issue throughout the crisis—the relation of church and state in the social order—their reactions to the papal condemnation differed because of political considerations of a different order. The rift was aggravated by Bernanos' violent attacks on Maritain's "capitulation" to Rome, and it was not mended until the midthirties.

The occasion for the reconciliation was the fact that Bernanos, who had originally supported Franco, began gradually to fall in line with Maritain's persistent neutrality on the issue of the Spanish Civil War. Bernanos published several articles at this time in *Sept,* the Catholic weekly with which Maritain had been so deeply involved, and in the years to come he was seen more frequently at Meudon, where he and Maritain appeared to have regained some of their former warmth. Although their differences over l'Action Française were never completely overcome, the two writers always had great respect for each other, and their thinking was very close on almost every other important issue.

The relationship between Maritain and François Mauriac was a long and fruitful one in which there were few if any significant misunderstandings. Before the crisis of l'Action Française, which awoke Maritain's latent social consciousness, their political persuasions were not very compatible. While Maritain was associated with Maurras and his ultraconservatives, Mauriac was a member of the extremist liberal movement known as *Le Sillon.*

Their agreement on the Spanish Civil War, however, brought them together in the 1930s, and the warmth of the friendship was firmly established from that time on.

As one might expect, the question of the Christian novelist's relation to evil was the point on which Maritain and Mauriac found themselves engaged in the most fruitful dialogue. Each had a considerable influence on the other's thinking, to the point that the famous phrase—"purify the source"—which they agreed was the best answer to the problem, was attributed by each to the other. Mauriac was strongly affected by *Art and Scholasticism, The Responsibility of the Artist,* and other books by Maritain on art. And Maritain often quoted from Mauriac's *God and Mammon (Dieu et Mammon,* 1958) and his personal writings. Their collaboration on *Sept,* on pamphlets during the turmoil of the 1930s, and at the Thomist meetings at Meudon helped deepen their mutual respect and affection. In his memoirs, Mauriac writes: "Jacques Maritain never ceased keeping an uneasy and sometimes anxious eye on me. But he did not attempt any direct intervention. He responded publicly to any call for help that escaped me. I had the certitude that he kept watch over my life."[13]

It has already been observed that Maritain showed himself to be greatly concerned with the new trends in the novel. His favorite novelist was a Russian, Dostoevski. But within French literature one of his dreams was to see the Catholic literary renaissance produce a great novelist in his own country. For a while his hopes rested with Bernanos, but the personal differences they experienced kept him from embracing Bernanos's work unreservedly. Mauriac he acknowledged as a writer of great power, but Mauriac appears to have portrayed sin in a somewhat indulgent light for Maritain's way of thinking. It appears now that his favorite contemporary French novelist was the French-American writer Julien Green. In a tribute to Green published just after the novelist's election to the French Academy, Maritain wrote: "I find it marvelous that an American should be the greatest writer of our time."[14]

The influence that Maritain had on Green was remarkably strong. Born into the Protestant faith, Green had converted to Catholicism in his adolescence but had grown away from the church because of his traumatic experiences with homosexuality. During his estrangement from the church, he became a great admirer and close friend of André Gide, who encouraged him to be more explicit in his writings concerning his erotic problems. In the 1930s, a period of time in which he gradually moved back toward regaining his faith, Julien Green seems to have found himself pulled in two different directions, represented by Gide and Maritain. The situation is a revealing example of the extent to which Gide and Maritain were rival forces in the world of French letters during the Meudon years. With André Breton, they were probably the most powerful writers to be looked upon as leaders among the literary establishment.

It was Maritain who repeatedly told Green, even during his years outside the church, that he was a man who lived essentially on a mystical plane and that his fictional world was not a purely human one. And his conversations with Green in 1939 were among the most important factors that led to Green's reconversion in that year. In his diary, Julien Green often refers to Maritain's physical appearance as angelic and acknowledges his great indebtedness to his old philosopher friend, as well as to Raïssa: "No one will ever quite know what their affection has meant to me. One of the greatest favors ever granted to me by God was to place Jacques on my path in 1924. I particularly want to say this."[15]

Among the poets whose names appear in lists of the Meudon faithful, one finds most frequent mention of Pierre Reverdy and Max Jacob. The greatest poet, for Maritain, was Dante, but these were the two contemporary French poets who most influenced his thinking. Jacob's aesthetic aphorisms are often quoted in *Art and Scholasticism* and *Creative Intuition in Art and Poetry,* and Reverdy's poems are among the more prominent ones included in the "texts without comment" in the latter work. Both Reverdy and Jacob were also involved in Maritain's efforts to bring Jean Cocteau back to Catholicism in 1925.

IX *Influence in America*

In the United States, Maritain found something of a second home. He felt strongly that his vocation had led him here, and that is why his presence in this country during World War II grew into something more than the temporary exile that was endured by other French intellectuals of the period. American philosophy, political and social thought, and theology all offered him a chance to make the Thomist revival felt. But the American literary scene was an especially intriguing context in which Maritain wanted to express himself.

The American poet of lasting importance whose work was most deeply influenced by Maritain was Allen Tate. Tate has said: "Jacques Maritain's influence on me was pervasive from the time I first knew him in 1940 until his death. . . . Jacques was a very great man. Not only a great intellect, but a warm and friendly human being who had he been a clergyman would no doubt be canonized."[16]

The critic Francis Fergusson, who knew Tate and Maritain quite well at Princeton, says that the influence was not only personal and spiritual in nature but also directly literary. In a personal interview, Fergusson said it was through Maritain that Tate read Aquinas. He added that "The Seasons of the Soul" was perhaps the clearest example of a direct literary influence. In this poem, he sees Tate as a much more philosophically and psychologically integrated poet freed from the morass of modern philosophical skepticism and gnosticism. And Tate himself, in "The Symbolic Imagination" and "The Angelic Imagination," acknowledges a great debt to Jacques and Raïssa Maritain in his thinking on the angelism of such poets as Edgar Allen Poe.

Fergusson's own writings have not escaped Maritain's influence. The major thrust of his criticism and art theory has been a basic revitalization of the modern perspective on art (since the great poetic revolution of the nineteenth century) through the use of Aristotle, Aquinas, Plato, and other ancients who seemed to have been too often neglected. He was already involved in this direction when he encountered Maritain's work, but Maritain did lead him further into Thomism—especially the French Thomists —and confirmed his interest in Aristotle. Fergusson also feels that Maritain was good at pointing out truths already vaguely perceived by the reader but never before so well articulated. He says that Maritain, for him, for Tate, and for many others, presented a philosophy that is very useful in finding one's way around in the modern world.

Another major American writer who was involved with this same group at Princeton was Tate's first wife, Caroline Gordon. Miss Gordon, too, still feels greatly indebted to Jacques Maritain as both a personal and literary influence. Her novel *The Male-factors* (1956) is dedicated to him, and her most recent book,

The Glory of Hera (1972), is based largely on *Art and Scholasticism,* in which she finds "the most profound and complete aesthetic of the novel." Miss Gordon is persuaded that many of Maritain's ideas are currently in circulation without being credited to him. "One of the things," she writes, "that most impressed me about Jacques was that he read novels as if he were a novelist, read poetry as if he were a poet and looked at pictures as if he were a painter. . . . Maritain knew more about the novel, I think, than anybody I have ever known."[17]

The tone of Mr. Fergusson's comments on this Princeton group attests to an unusually happy meeting of minds. Fergusson, Tate, Gordon, and Maritain were all traditionalists by temperament. The critic, the poet, the novelist, and the philosopher of art—they complemented each other's work most effectively. And they all found a well-articulated philosophy to serve as a foundation for their diverse fields in Maritain's Thomism.

T.S. Eliot also had considerable contact with Maritain at Princeton, but his reaction to Maritain's philosophy was altogether different. In this he betrayed the more typically British side of his character. Although he called Maritain "probably the greatest force in contemporary French philosophy," Aristotelianism and Thomism were too rigidly systematic for Eliot's taste. Robert Speaight, the British actor whose literary biographies (Bernanos, Mauriac, etc.) have a widespread public among students of French literature, believes that Maritain's influence on Eliot was considerable. Other British writers whom he cites as having been marked by Maritain's Thomist aesthetic include himself, Eric Gill, Herbert Read, and Bernard Wall. In general, however, the English literati appeared to regard Maritain's literary importance as more of an American phenomenon. The political theories of Maritain were less acceptable to most English Catholics, who seemed to prefer the philosophy of Gabriel Marcel.

Maritain's teaching and writing in Canada have left a lasting impression in that country, too. Morley Callaghan and Marshall McLuhan are two examples of the Canadian connection, which was obviously enhanced by the career of Etienne Gilson. And the foremost Maritain translator in the United States, Joseph W. Evans, is Canadian by birth and education.

The remarkable careers of John Howard Griffin and Thomas Merton have also been deeply touched by Jacques Maritain.

Griffin's case is illustrative of other American Catholics' attitude toward Maritain in that he finds it "difficult to separate the aesthetic from the overall philosophical picture. . . With me it is deeply mixed with the ethical."[18] Griffin has referred to his controversial book, *Black Like Me* (1961), as a "living out" of Maritain's ideas on racism, and he adds that his aesthetic ideas are drawn directly from Maritain. In Griffin's *Jacques Maritain: Homage in Words and Pictures* (1974), a most fascinating chapter concerns the last reunion of Maritain and Merton at the latter's hermitage near the Trappist monastery in Gethsemani, Kentucky. Thomas Merton attributed his conversion to Gilson and Maritain, and his whole conception of the world was immersed in the scholastic philosophy that has been revitalized and brought to bear once more on the realities of modern life by those two Thomists. Maritain's aesthetics and his thinking on the relationship of art and morality were important for Merton as early as the time of his graduate research on William Blake. Such notions as the connatural knowledge of the artist and art as a virtue of the practical intellect excited his imagination and opened up new interpretations of Blake's poetry. The more personal questions of art and faith in his own life, in turn, began to reveal themselves in a new light.

The complete list of writers whose life and art have been touched by Jacques Maritain would undoubtedly reach astonishingly far. The foregoing represents a cursory glance at a topic that could prove extremely fertile for a more detailed investigation. Hopefully, it conveys some idea of what Maritain's meditations on the situation of the artist have meant to the modern literary worlds of France and the United States.

CHAPTER 11

Conclusion

A T times, the prose of Maritain is complicated, his sentences lengthy and involuted. Despite Maritain's obvious natural gift for elegant style, one must be prepared to make a concentrated effort in order to follow the philosopher's line of thought. The intellectual toughness of reading Maritain is due mainly, however, to the nature of his subject and to the intricacies of the scholastic method that he so faithfully followed. Most books he wrote for the public at large are exceptionally lucid articulations of philosophical truths. Among the best examples of Maritain's ability to state his philosophy in clear language accessible to the serious layman are the shorter books published during his American residence: essays like *On the Use of Philosophy* and *The Responsibility of the Artist,* which originated, for the most part, as lectures at American universities.

W.K. Wimsatt is right in saying that Maritain's propositions on art "have the ring of that kind of inevitable truth that approximates truism. They are universals of sensitive introspection and metaphysical deduction."[1]

In reading Maritain's philosophy, a layman may at times feel somewhat lost and not so sure of the direction in which he is being led. But once the argument has culminated in conclusions, the reader feels the limpid self-evidence of Maritain's pronouncements. They seem so undeniable that it is difficult to imagine how the philosopher arrived at them through such lengthy reasoning—reasoning that, however, adds weight to the conviction of certainty that one feels for them. Witness the following description of the metaphysical reality of being: "It is something primordial, at once very simple and very rich, and, if you will, inexpressible in the sense that it is that whose perception is the most difficult to describe, because it is the most immediate" (PM, 52 - 53).

There is, indeed, a strong lyrical strain in the prose of

156

Maritain. It deepens one's understanding of the truths to which he gives expression. He feels the intuitive force of those truths to such a profound degree that they often burst forth onto the page in lines of admirable grace. His style, at its best, places him in a tradition of great French thinkers—those who have felt most keenly the characteristically French conviction that a philosophy can endure only to the extent that its expression achieves aesthetic excellence.

If Maritain's prose is sometimes difficult to follow, it may also be understood in part as a result of the itinerary that most of his works have followed in order to reach publication in book form. As a rule, he began with a lecture or series of lectures delivered in somewhat less formal style. These lectures usually appeared in revised form as articles in various reviews and journals. Ultimately, they were compiled under appropriate titles and published as books. Seldom did Maritain have the opportunity to set himself about writing a book as a unified work, and for this reason many of his books are lacking, to a certain degree, in organization and unity. A notable exception is *Art and Scholasticism,* which he wrote in its entirety during an extended illness of his wife Raïssa.

A side effect of the seemingly disorganized coming together of fragments into book form is that a good many articles or lectures appear in more than one book. Moreover, Maritain has shown a persistent tendency to revise and add to his work in later editions. As a result, he often returns to old themes with a freshness of approach that bespeaks the living quality of his thought. Maritain's books thus overlap and explain each other because of the fundamental unity imparted to them by their organic growth. For Maritain, philosophy, and especially Thomist philosophy, should never be thought of as rigid and static. Thomism "is not a system, an artifact; it is a spiritual organism," he wrote in *The Degrees of Knowledge.* Thomism is not an essentially medieval philosophy adapted and "applied" to the contemporary world, and for this reason Maritain always resented the label "*Neo*-Thomism."

With Maritain's death in April of 1973, it was as if the last living remnant of an era in the intellectual life of France had finally disappeared. In a way it seemed that he had outlived his own time, what with the widespread disenchantment that had greeted his last controversial book, *The Peasant of the Garonne.*

Certainly, his influence during the last ten to twelve years of his life could not be said to rival his importance in France between the two wars, when so many prominent French intellectuals were still finding authentic spiritual nourishment in the Catholic faith. Maritain seemed to observe the contemporary intellectual and artistic trends from afar, isolated in his monastic retreat outside Toulouse.

But if one examines the content of Maritain's writings during his retreat with the Little Brothers of Jesus, one finds not only a series of philosophical treatments of metaphysical and theological questions, but also a considerable amount of material devoted to the most pressing current problems of the secular world. As he did so often throughout his career, Maritain—even into the tenth decade of his life and from a remote place of solitude—was reaffirming the living, dynamic realism of his beloved Thomist philosophy. In his *On the Church of Christ* (1970), for example, he writes not only of the church's attitude toward historical events such as the trials of Galileo and Joan of Arc, but also of her proper relation to contemporary issues such as the state of Israel, the adherents of Communism, and even the hippies. Indeed, his remarks on the students of the 1968 revolt and on the trends of the contemporary world's youth in general are penetrating and useful.

In France today, it is said that any book written about God is assured of an immense popularity. While it would not be accurate to attribute such a state of affairs to one man's writings, it would be equally inept to discount Maritain's influence on the modern scene. He and Teilhard de Chardin are the two thinkers most likely to have created such a widespread interest in theology in France.

Those who knew Jacques Maritain invariably find it hard to talk about his influence without acknowledging the effect that his life had on them. Apparently, he never lost sight of his double role as contemplative and as witness to the philosophy that he professed in his writings. As a writer, he made his most significant achievements in the fields of political and social philosophy, aesthetics and criticism. But another hallmark of his work is the extraordinary diversity of the fields of knowledge into which he carried the Thomist perspective. The basis for speculative philosophy, which he found in the Aristotelian-Thomist metaphysics, proved fruitful not only in art and politics but in theology, history, education, and even science. And one of the most valuable contributions he made to modern culture was his vision of the fundamental unity of all the fields of knowledge—fields that have been severed one from the other in the compartmentalized version of knowledge offered by modern scholars. It is a thing of great value for contemporary students and thinkers to be shown that the artist and the nuclear physicist, for example, approach the same basic mystery of life in their own ways.

Maritain was indeed a man of paradoxes. He had a tender, sensitive heart that was forever wary of offending others, but in his writings he was capable of the deadliest assualts on ideas. Born and reared in a fiercely anticlerical family, he ended his life in the novitiate of a Dominican monastic order. His philosophy, based almost totally on the writings of a man who lived in the twelfth century, was focused on the most immediate issues of contemporary culture. He was a Frenchman who always felt a great love for his country and for his native tongue, and yet he wrote some of his greatest books in English.

In attempting to sum up the unique thrust of Maritain's thought, one would have to point to the central paradox of his deep interest in the philosophy of the ancients and the cultural movements of the modern world. For Maritain's greatest achievement was the forging of a synthesis, one that was earlier compared to Thomas Aquinas's synthesis of Aristotle and Christian doctrine. In returning to the fountainhead of Western thought—Aristotle, Plato, Aquinas—Maritain revived the modern world's understanding of the ancients and brought a new perspective to the currents of civilization in which he lived. The course of Western philosophy, political and social thought, and aesthetic theory all bear the mark of Jacques Maritain: antimodern, peasant of the Garonne, pilgrim of the absolute, philosopher of art, and artist of philosophy.

Notes and References

Chapter One

1. Nicolai Berdiaev, *Essai d'autobiographie spirituelle*, trans. [from Russian] E. Belenson (Paris, 1958), p. 331 (my translation).
2. Raïssa Maritain, *Raïssa's Journal* (Albany, 1974), pp. 235 - 36.
3. *Approches sans entraves* (Paris, 1973), p. 52 (my translation).
4. *Carnet de notes* (Paris, 1965), pp. 16 - 17 (my translation).
5. Raïssa Maritain, *Adventures in Grace,* trans. Julie Kernan (New York, 1945), pp. 213 - 15.
6. *Ibid.,* p. 214.
7. John Howard Griffin and Yves R. Simon, *Jacques Maritain: Homage in Words and Pictures* (Albany, 1974), p. 52.
8. "Pilgrim of the Absolute," *Time,* May 14, 1973, p. 85.

Chapter Two

1. *A Preface to Metaphysics: Seven Lectures on Being* (New York, 1939). References to this text will use the abbreviation PM.
2. Julien Green, *To Leave Before Dawn,* trans. Anne Green (New York, 1967), p. 13.

Chapter Three

1. *Distinguish to Unite: or, The Degrees of Knowledge,* trans. Gerald B. Phelan (New York, 1959). References to this text will use the abbreviation DK.

Chapter Four

1. *Philosophy of Nature,* trans. Imelda C. Byrne (New York, 1951). References to this text will use the abbreviation PN.
2. Emile Meyerson, *De l'explication dans les sciences* (Paris, 1921), vol. I, p. 6.
3. *Approches sans entraves* (Paris, 1973), p. 113. The translation not being available, all quotes from this text are my translations.
4. *Ibid.,* p. 157.
5. *Ibid.,* p. 132.
6. *Ibid.,* p. 148.

Chapter Five

1. *Freedom in the Modern World,* trans. Richard O'Sullivan (New York, 1936), p. 145.
2. *Humanisme intégral: problèmes temporels et spirituels d'une nouvelle chrétienté* (Paris, 1936).
3. *Integral Humanism: Temporal and Spiritual Problems of a New Christendom,* trans. Joseph W. Evans (New York, 1968). References to this text will use the abbreviation IH.
4. *Man and the State* (Chicago, 1951), p. 34. References to this text will use the abbreviation MS.
5. *Reflections on America* (New York, 1958), p. 175. References to this text will use the abbreviation REF.

Chapter Six

1. *Education at the Crossroads* (New Haven, 1943). References to this text will use the abbreviation EC.
2. J. Maritain, *The Education of Man,* ed. Donald and Idella Gallagher (Garden City, 1962), p. 82. References to this text will use the abbreviation EM.

Chapter Seven

1. *On the Philosophy of History* (New York, 1957). References to this text will use the abbreviation PH.
2. *Existence and the Existent,* trans. Lewis Galantière and Gerald B. Phelan (New York, 1948), pp. 85 - 122.

Chapter Eight

1. These famous letters are available in English under the title *Art and Faith,* trans. John Coleman (New York, 1948).
2. *Art and Scholasticism and The Frontiers of Poetry,* trans. Joseph W. Evans (New York, 1962). References to this text will use the abbreviation AS.
3. Quoted in *Creative Intuition in Art and Poetry* (New York, 1953), p. 58. References to this text will use the abbreviation CI.
4. *The Responsibility of the Artist* (New York, 1960), p. 37. References to this text will use the abbreviation RA.
5. "Poi chi pinge figura,/Se non può essere lei, non la può porre." *Convivio,* IV, Canzone 52 - 53.
6. Francis Fergusson, *The Idea of a Theatre* (Princeton, 1949), p. 4.
7. *Art and Faith,* p. 74.

8. *Art and Poetry,* trans. Elva de Pue Matthews (New York, 1943), p. 53.

Chapter Nine

1. *The Peasant of the Garonne: An Old Layman Questions Himself about the Present Time,* trans. M. Cuddihy and E. Hughes (New York, 1968). References to this text will use the abbreviation PG.

2. "L'élite de notre jeunesse cherche—et trouvera—des raisons de vivre," *Le Figaro littéraire,* 31 mars - 6 avril, 1969, pp. 6 - 7.

3. Quoted in *The Peasant of the Garonne,* p. 189.

Chapter Ten

1. Bloy, too, influenced Maritain's thinking on the Jews in a different way. His *Le Salut par les Juifs* gave Maritain a theological understanding of the role of the children of Israel in the divine plan. Péguy, on the other hand, fought anti-Semitism solely as a social phenomenon, without according the Jews any particular theological significance. (For a comprehensive discussion of Maritain and the Jewish question, see Bernard Doering's dissertation, *Jacques Maritain and French Literary Figures in the Political and Social Turmoil of 1920 - 1950,* ch. 5 [Ph.D., Colorado, 1967]).

2. The only exception was the eldest son, Marcel, who became a Methodist.

3. *Adventures in Grace,* p. 304.

4. "Henri Bergson," *Commonweal,* XXXIII (January 17, 1941), 317 - 19; and "Subject of Bergson's Christianity," *Commonweal,* XXXIV (August 29, 1941), 446.

5. *Adventures in Grace,* p. 198.

6. Péguy and Bloy are comparable on several counts, but Maritain was never to bring the two together, partly because of Mme Favre-Maritain's resentment toward Bloy, with which she seems to have prejudiced Péguy, and partly because of Péguy's fierce intellectual independence, which he felt threatened by Bloy.

7. *Adventures in Grace,* pp. 27 - 28.

8. Helen Iswolski, *Light Before Dusk: A Russian Catholic in France, 1923 - 1941* (New York, 1942), pp. 91 - 100.

9. Henri Bars, *Maritain en notre temps* (Paris, 1959), p. 100.

10. Harry Stuart Hughes, *The Obstructed Path: French Social Thought in the Years of Desperation, 1930 - 1960* (New York, 1968), pp. 72 - 96.

11. "Rencontres," *La Revue de Paris,* September 1953, pp. 31 - 35.

12. Georges Guy-Grand, *André Gide et notre temps* (Paris, 1935), p. 47 (my translation).

13. François Mauriac, *The Inner Presence,* trans. Herma Briffault (Indianapolis, 1968).

14. "Je trouve merveilleux qu'un Américain soit le plus grand écrivain de notre temps." "Fidélité à l'esprit," *Renaissance de Fleury,* 19e année, no. 75 (octobre 1970), 13 (my translation).

15. Julien Green, *Diary 1928 - 1957,* trans. Anne Green (New York, 1964), p. 278.

16. Letter to the author, May 4, 1976.

17. Letter to the author, July 25, 1976.

18. Letter to the author, July 5, 1976.

Chapter Eleven

1. W.K. Wimsatt, "Gay in the Mystery," *Poetry,* 87 (February 1956), 309.

Selected Bibliography

PRIMARY SOURCES

1. Original Editions
(Except where indicated otherwise, place of publication is Paris.)

La Philosophie bergsonienne: études critiques. Marcel Rivière et Cie., 1914.

Art et Scolastique. Librairie de l'Art Catholique, 1920. (The 1927 edition by Louis Rouart et Fils also contains "Frontières de la Poésie" and important notes.)

Antimoderne. Editions de la Revue des Jeunes, 1922.

Trois Réformateurs: Luther, Descartes, Rousseau. Librairie Plon, 1925.

Georges Rouault, peintre et lithographe. Editions Polyglotte, Frapier, 1926.

Réponse à Jean Cocteau. Librairie Stock, 1926.

Primauté du spirituel. Librairie Plon, 1927.

Le Docteur angélique. Desclée de Brouwer, 1930.

Distinguer pour unir: ou, les degrés du savoir. Desclée de Brouwer, 1932.

Du Régime temporel et de la liberté. Desclée de Brouwer, 1933.

Sept leçons sur l'être et les premiers principes de la raison spéculative. Pierre Téqui, 1934.

Lettre sur l'indépendance. Desclée de Brouwer, 1935.

La Philosophie de la nature, essai critique sur ses frontières et son objet. Pierre Téqui, 1935.

Humanisme intégral: problèmes temporels et spirituels d'une nouvelle chrétienté. Fernand Aubier, 1936.

Situation de la poésie. Desclée de Brouwer, 1938. (In collaboration with Raïssa Maritain.)

Les Juifs parmi les nations. Editions du cerf, 1938.

A travers le désastre. New York: Editions de la Maison Française, 1941.

La Pensée de Saint Paul, textes choisis et présentés. New York: Editions de la Maison Française, 1941.

Les Droits de l'homme et la loi naturelle. New York: Editions de la Maison Française, 1942.

Christianisme et Démocratie. New York: Editions de la Maison Française, 1943.

Education at the Crossroads. New Haven: Yale University Press, 1943.

Court traité de l'existence et de l'existant. Paul Hartmann, 1947.

La Personne et le bien commun. Desclée de Brouwer, 1947.

Man and the State. Chicago: University of Chicago Press, 1951.

Creative Intuition in Art and Poetry. New York: Pantheon Books, 1953.

On the Philosophy of History. New York: Charles Scribner's Sons, 1957. (Four lectures transcribed from recordings and edited by Joseph W. Evans.)

Reflections on America. New York: Charles Scribner's Sons, 1958.

The Responsibility of the Artist. New York: Charles Scribner's Sons, 1960.

The Education of Man. Edited by Donald and Idella Gallagher. New York: Doubleday and Co., 1962.

Carnet de notes. Desclée de Brouwer, 1965.

Le Paysan de la Garonne: Un vieux laïc s'interroge à propos du temps présent. Desclée de Brouwer, 1967.

De la Grâce et de l'humanité de Jésus. Desclée de Brouwer, 1967.

De l'église du Christ, la Personne de l'Eglise et son personnel. Desclée de Brouwer, 1970.

Approches sans entraves. Librairie Arthème Fayard, 1973.

2. Translations

Three Reformers: Luther, Descartes, Rousseau (Trois Réformateurs: Luther, Descartes, Rousseau). New York: Charles Scribner's Sons, 1929.

The Things That Are Not Caesar's (Primauté du spirituel). New York: Charles Scribner's Sons, 1930. (Tr. J. F. Scanlan)

Freedom in the Modern World (Du Régime temporal et de la liberté). New York: Charles Scribner's Sons, 1936. (Tr. Richard O'Sullivan)

A Christian Looks at the Jewish Question (Les Juifs parmi les nations). New York: Longmans, Green, 1939.

A Preface to Metaphysics: Seven Lectures on Being (Sept leçons sur l'être et les premiers principes de la raison spéculative). New York and London: Sheed and Ward, 1939.

Ransoming the Time. New York: Charles Scribner's Sons, 1941. (These essays were translated from the French by Harry Lorin Binsse, but there is no French counterpart to this volume in which all the essays are gathered.)

France, My Country, Through the Disaster (A travers le désastre). New York: Longmans, Green, 1941.

Art and Poetry. New York: Philosophical Library, 1943. (A translation, by E. de P. Matthews, of "Trois Peintres," "Dialogues," and "La Clef des chants," published in *Frontières de la poésie.)*

The Living Thoughts of Saint Paul (La Pensée de Saint Paul, textes choisis et présentés). New York: Longmans, Green, 1941. (Tr. Harry Lorin Binsse)

The Rights of Man and Natural Law (Les Droits de l'homme et la loi naturelle). New York: Charles Scribner's Sons, 1943. (Tr. Doris C. Anson)

Christianity and Democracy (Christianisme et Démocratie). New York:

Scribner's 1944. (Tr. Doris C. Anson)

The Person and the Common Good (La Personne et le bien commun).
New York: Charles Scribner's Sons, 1947. (Tr. John J.
Fitzgerald)

*Art and Faith: Letters Between Jacques Maritain and Jean Cocteau
(Réponse à Jean Cocteau)*. New York: Philosophical Library, 1948.
(Tr. John Coleman; also includes Cocteau's *Lettre à Jacques
Maritain*, cited below)

Existence and the Existent (Court traité de l'existence et de l'existant).
New York: Pantheon Books, 1948. (Tr. Lewis Galantière and
Gerald B. Phelan)

*Philosophy of Nature (La Philosophie de la nature, essai critique sur ses
frontières et son objet)*. New York: Philosophical Library, 1951.
(Tr. Imelda C. Byrne)

Georges Rouault (Georges Rouault, peintre et lithographe). New York:
Harry N. Abrams, Inc., in association with Pocket Books, Inc.,
1954.

*Bergsonian Philosophy and Thomism (La Philosophie bergsonienne:
études critiques)*. New York: Philosophical Library, 1955. (Tr.
Mabelle L. Andison with J. Gordon Andison)

The Situation of Poetry (Situation de la poésie). New York: Philosophical Library, 1955. (Tr. Marshall Suther)

St. Thomas Aquinas (Le Docteur angélique). New York: Meridian
Books, 1958. (Tr. and revised by Peter O'Reilly and Joseph W.
Evans)

*Distinguish to Unite: or, The Degrees of Knowledge (Distinguer pour
unir: ou, les degrés du savoir)*. New York: Charles Scribner's Sons,
1959. (Tr. under supervision of G. B. Phelan; much better than
earlier translations of this work)

Art and Scholasticism and The Frontiers of Poetry (Art et Scolastique).
New York: Charles Scribner's Sons, 1962. (Tr. Joseph W. Evans;
much better than earlier translations; also includes new material)

*Integral Humanism: Temporal and Spiritual Problems of a New
Christendom (Humanisme intégral: Problèmes temporels et spirituels d'une nouvelle chrétienté)*. New York: Charles Scribner's Sons,
1968. (Tr. Joseph W. Evans: by far superior to earlier translations
of this work)

*The Peasant of the Garonne: An Old Layman Questions Himself about
the Present Time (Le Paysan de la Garonne: un vieux laïc
s'interroge sur le temps présent)*. New York: Holt, Rinehart, and
Winston, 1968. (Tr. Michael Cuddihy and Elizabeth Hughes)

*On the Grace and Humanity of Jesus (De le Grâce et de l'humanité de
Jésus)*. New York: Herder and Herder, 1969. (Tr. Joseph W. Evans)

*On the Church of Christ: The Person of the Church and Her Personnel
(De l'église du Christ: La Personne de l'Eglise et son personnel)*.
Notre Dame, Indiana: University of Notre Dame Press, 1973. (Tr.
Joseph W. Evans)

SECONDARY SOURCES

1. Books or Portions of Books on Maritain

ALLEN, EDGAR LEONARD. *Christian Humanism: A Guide to the Thought of Jacques Maritain.* New York: Philosophical Library, 1951. Short, well-organized summary, but often too narrowly Catholic in point of view.

BARS, HENRI. *Maritain en notre temps.* Bernard Grasset, 1959. Undoubtedly the best known study in French. Sound critical evaluation.

COCTEAU, JEAN. *Lettre à Jacques Maritain.* Librairie Stock, 1926. (Translation listed above as *Art and Faith: Letters Between Jacques Maritain and Jean Cocteau)* Unique document on one of the more notable events of the Catholic renaissance in France.

EVANS, JOSEPH W., ed. *Jacques Maritain: The Man and His Achievement.* New York. Sheed and Ward, 1963. Excellent collection of essays on diverse aspects of Maritain's work.

FECHER, CHARLES A. *The Philosophy of Jacques Maritain.* Westminister, Maryland: Newman Press, 1953. Useful layman's perspective, although somewhat rambling.

FOWLIE, WALLACE. "Maritain: The Message of a Philosopher." In *Jacob's Night: The Religious Renascence in France,* pp. 53 - 76. New York: Sheed and Ward, 1947. Maritain in the context of the French literary scene, especially during the Meudon years.

GALLAGHER, DONALD and IDELLA. *The Achievement of Jacques and Raïssa Maritain: A Bibliography, 1906 - 1961.* Garden City, New York: Doubleday and Co., Inc., 1962. A definitive bibliography of all works up to 1961.

GRIFFIN, JOHN HOWARD, and YVES R. SIMON. *Jacques Maritain: Homage in Words and Pictures.* Albany, New York: Magi Books, 1974. Very beautiful collection of Griffin's photographs of Maritain, along with entries from Griffin's diary concerning visits with Maritain in his last years. Also includes reprint of an important essay by Simon.

HOOK, SIDNEY. "Integral Humanism," In *Reason, Social Myths, and Democracy,* pp. 76 - 104. New York: The John Day Co., 1940. Bitterly critical of Maritain's sociopolitical theories.

ISWOLSKY, HELEN. "The House in Meudon" and "The Philosopher in the World." In *Light Before Dusk: A Russian Catholic in France, 1923 - 1941,* pp. 70 - 87, 184 - 99. New York: Longmans, Green, and Co., 1942. Important data on the Meudon days. Personal reminiscences of the philosophical dramas of the period.

KERNAN, JULIE. *Our Friend, Jacques Maritain: A Personal Memoir.* Garden City, New York: Doubleday and Co., Inc., 1975. The most complete existing biographical account.

MARITAIN, RAÏSSA. *Les Grandes Amitiés: Souvenirs.* New York: Editions de la Maison Française, 1941. *(We Have Been Friends Together,* tr. Julie Kernan. New York: Longmans, Green, and Co., 1942.) A wealth of biographical material on the Maritains' early lives up to ca. 1913.

——*Les Grandes Amitiés: les adventures de la grace.* New York: Editions de la Maison Française, 1944 *(Adventures in Grace,* tr. Julie Kernan. New York and Toronto: Longmans, Green, and Co., 1945.) Sequel to the above.

——*Le Journal de Raïssa.* Desclée de Brouwer, 1963. (Tr. *Raïssa's Journal.* Albany, New York: Magi Books, 1974.) The spiritual journey of a deeply contemplative woman. Also contains occasional valuable details on Jacques' life and career.

NOTTINGHAM, WILLIAM J. *Christian Faith and Secular Action: An Introduction to the Life and Thought of Jacques Maritain.* St. Louis: The Bethany Press, 1968. A sympthetic presentation of Maritain's Christian humanism, leading to Vactican II.

PHELAN, GERALD B. *Jacques Maritain.* New York: Sheed and Ward, 1937. One of the early authorities on Maritain. Solid, but very brief; lacks scope.

PSICHARI, HENRIETTE. *Les Convertis de la belle époque.* Paris: Editions rationalistes, 1971. Fiercely antagonistic toward the Catholic renaissance in France. Written by the staunchly atheist sister of Ernest Psichari.

2. Articles on Maritain

BRAZZOLA, GEORGES. "Introduction à la poétique de Jacques Maritain." *La Table Ronde,* January 1959, pp. 62 - 66.

CLANCY, WILLIAM P. "The Intuition of Jacques Maritain." *The Commonweal,* December 25, 1953, pp. 309 - 10.

CLANCY, WILLIAM P. and KENNETH REXROTH. "Peasant of the Garonne: Two Views." *The Commonweal,* April 12, 1968, pp. 106 - 10.

COCTEAU, JEAN. "Rencontres." *La Revue de Paris,* September 1953, pp. 31 - 35. Personal memories of Maritain.

COLLINS, JAMES. "Maritain the Philosopher—The Defender of Human Intelligence." *The Commonweal,* June 11, 1954, pp. 246 - 49. General essay—very well done.

——"Maritain Asks Some Questions." *America,* January 13, 1968, pp. 29-32. On *The Peasant of the Garonne.*

FRANK, JOSEPH. "Maritain's View of Modern Art." *The New Republic,* May 30, 1955, pp. 17 - 18. On *Creative Intuition in Art and Poetry.*

HUGHES, H. STUART. "Marcel, Maritain and the Secular World," *The American Scholar,* Autumn 1966, pp. 728 - 49. Excellent comparison of Gabriel Marcel and Maritain.

MCLUHAN, H. MARSHALL. "Maritain on Art." *Renascence,* Autumn 1953, pp. 40 - 44. On *Creative Intuition in Art and Poetry.*

"Pilgrim of the Absolute." *Time,* May 14, 1973, pp. 85 - 86. Obituary tribute.

"Teacher of the Pope." *Time,* April 21, 1967, p. 69. On Vatican II, Maritain's friendship with Paul VI, and *The Peasant of the Garonne.*

WHITMAN, ALDEN. "Jacques Maritain, Philosopher, Dies." *The New York Times,* April 29, 1973, p. 60. Obituary article—good retrospective biographical summary.

WIMSATT, W. K. JR. "Gay in the Mystery." *Poetry,* 87 (February 1956), 308 - 11. On *Creative Intuition in Art and Poetry.*

Index

(The works of Maritain are listed under his name)

171